To my grandchildren Maggie and Robert
and all the other grandchildren who deserve
to inherit an America that is as free, safe, healthy
and prosperous as the America we inherited

and

To the millions of Americans (including first
generation immigrants who want to become American)
who will have to work, argue, struggle and at times fight
to preserve our freedom, our safety, our health
and our prosperity.

WINNING THE FUTURE

A 21ST CENTURY CONTRACT WITH AMERICA

NEWT GINGRICH

Library of Congress Cataloging-in-Publication Data on file with the Library of Congress

ISBN 0-89526-042-5

Published in the United States by
Regnery Publishing, Inc.
An Eagle Publishing Company
One Massachusetts Avenue, NW
Washington, DC 20001
Visit us at www.regnery.com

Distributed to the trade by
National Book Network
4720-A Boston Way
Lanham, MD 20706

Printed on acid-free paper

Manufactured in the United States of America

10 9 8 7 6 5 4 3 2 1

Contents

Test Yourself

WHERE DO YOU STAND on the great and growing gap between traditional American values and the secular liberalism of the Left? Take the following test.

Score each statement from 1 to 10 depending on how much you agree or disagree with it, with 10 meaning you strongly agree and 1 meaning you strongly disagree. If you're neutral, write 5. Add the score at the end. The higher the score, the more you lean toward traditional American values. The lower the score, the more you favor the secular left-liberal system. The percentages next to each question are recent poll numbers that reflect public opinion on the issue.

___ 1 We should be allowed to say "one nation under God" in the Pledge of Allegiance. (91 percent of Americans agree)

___ 2 Able-bodied people on welfare should be required to work. (87 percent agree)

___ 3 Men who assault pregnant women and kill the unborn child should be prosecuted for assault and murder. (84 percent agree)

___ 4 The United States should put its own interests first and cooperation with international organizations second. (73 percent agree)

___ 5 Believe in God. (92 percent agree)

___ 6 Proud to be an American. (91 percent agree)

___ 7 Schools should teach new immigrants about American values. (88 percent agree)

___ 8 Everyone should learn English. (81 percent agree)

___ 9 Personal injury lawyers should get no more than 15 percent of any award. (75 percent agree)

___ 10 It is possible to use new technology and new science to develop clean, renewable energy that protects the environment and the economy. (88 percent agree)

Add up your score. If you scored above 51 points, read on. This book is about how you can protect and defend America's traditions and values.

INTRODUCTION

Our Generation's Rendezvous with Destiny

OUR GENERATION OF AMERICANS received the most blessed inheritance in history. Our parents and grandparents endured the Great Depression, fought the Second World War, contained the Soviet Union, and helped the people of Western Europe, Japan, and South Korea achieve unimagined levels of prosperity. They went to school, took extra jobs, and started businesses. They created a level of prosperity unknown to any other people in history. Out of their idealism they ended segregation. They maintained an open door so that an Austrian-born American could be governor of California and other first generation immigrants could win the Nobel Prize, serve as secretary of state, build companies, create jobs, and enrich our lives in America.

Our generation inherited all of these wonderful things. But what will be *our* legacy? We are now entering a decade that will test our own courage, persistence, and resolve, a decade that will be what Franklin Delano Roosevelt called our generation's rendezvous with destiny.

I write these words as someone who spent twenty years in the United States House of Representatives and who has made a lifelong study—including a Ph.D.—of history. Moreover, since I left government in January 1999, I have made an in-depth study of national security, health, science and technology, and the American economy. I have had the unusual experience of being an academic, a leader at the center of government power, and now a student of Washington using both those tools: the academic and the practical.

What I have learned since leaving the Speakership is not reassuring.

The Threats to America's Future

Today America is vulnerable to five threats that, taken collectively, are as daunting and difficult as any America has faced. Four of them could undermine, even eliminate, America as we know it, while the fifth could leave us weakened, impoverished, and with much less freedom. The rising threats are:

1. That Islamic terrorists and rogue dictatorships will acquire and launch nuclear or biological weapons.
2. That God will be driven from American public life and reduce us to the civilizational ennui that now characterizes a declining Europe.
3. That America will lose the patriotic sense of itself as a unique civilization.
4. That America's economic supremacy will yield to China and India because of failing schools and weakening scientific and technological leadership.
5. That an aging America's demands on Social Security, Medicare, and related government programs will collapse the system.

These five threats are real and dangerous. If they are not met and solved, they will cripple our nation. Each threat can be overcome, but standing in our way is an entrenched political system and news media that refuse to confront these threats seriously.

Who We Are; Who Our Opponents Are

Traditional politics is dominated by and defined by a collection of elites who are deeply opposed to the solutions America needs to renew its civilization and ensure its economic and national security interests. These elites want a dramatically different world from the values and aspirations of most Americans. Consider just a few examples of the chasm that exists between the two sides.

Most of us believe that 9/11 was enough proof that we have enemies who hate us and who would kill millions of Americans if given the chance. Yet our national security bureaucracies continue to operate within a peacetime model. Our liberal national security elites believe that we should defend America only within the framework of an ineffective United Nations and the approval of a skeptical Europe.

Most of us believe that America was founded as a nation in which people are "endowed by our Creator with certain inalienable rights" and that we rightly pledge allegiance to "one nation under God." But an arrogant judiciary increasingly tries to drive God from public life.

Most of us believe that America is a good and decent country created by heroes worth studying. But the schools that teach young Americans and American immigrants offer politically correct, multicultural drivel, fail to teach American history, and ridicule what little they are forced to teach.

Over the last four decades, America has been divided into these two camps. In the first are those elites who find it acceptable to drive God out of public life and who, in general, also scorn American history, support economic regulation over freedom and competition, favor a "sophisticated" foreign policy led by the United Nations, and agree with the *New York Times*.

But Americans in the other camp who are proud of our history know how integral God is to understanding American exceptionalism, know how vital the creative and competitive spirit is to being American, and believe that America is worth defending even if it irritates foreigners who do not share our values. In Samuel Huntington's book, *Who Are We? The Challenges to America's National Identity*, he points out that 85 percent of Americans are proud of their institutions,[1] 78 percent believe children should be allowed to pray in school, and 87 percent take pride in their work.[2] Only 23 percent of Americans believe the United Nations should play a leading role in world affairs and have countries defer to its policies.[3]

Most of us believe in doing the hard work that will keep America's economy second to none. But our efforts are hampered by trial lawyers who seek their own enrichment instead of justice; by labor unions that insist on special deals and protection instead of competition; and by bureaucracies that emphasize process over achievement.

Self-government implies that on these issues, the people should rule, but the liberal elite minority is winning and the popular majority is losing. Since the 1960s, the conservative majority has been intimidated, manipulated, and bullied by the liberal minority. The liberal elites who dominate academia, the courts, the press, and much of the government bureaucracy share an essentially European secular-socialist value system. Yet they have set the terms of the debate, which is why "politics as usual" is a losing proposition for Americans.

Politics as History

We need to replace "politics as usual" with "politics as history," so that we focus on the long term, face facts, and act on them. In fact, this process has been the populist corrective action throughout American history.

In the 1790s, Thomas Jefferson and James Madison founded a political party to wrest power from the aristocratic Federalists and enact populist change. In 1800 they won a decisive victory and within fifteen years the Federalists had disappeared. One of the boldest acts of the Jeffersonians was to abolish the old judgeships and assert the right to correct the Supreme Court if it misinterpreted the Constitution, a fight that needs to be renewed.

In 1824, American populists felt that the presidency had been stolen from their hero, General Andrew Jackson, by a collection of corrupt, rich Easterners. In a savage four-year campaign, the populists destroyed the presidency of John Quincy Adams and swept the country for a Jacksonian majority. The Jacksonians reformed federal institutions and brought true, grassroots democracy back to America.

In 1857, the *Dred Scott* decision by the Supreme Court threatened to legalize the expansion of slavery. The new Republican Party, which had run its first presidential campaign in 1856, was energized by the opposition to this decision, and in 1860, it won the presidency. President Abraham Lincoln, who led the Republicans, was a genuine revolutionary. With courage and tenacity, he did what it took to restore a fractured Union and end the wrong of slavery.

At the turn of the century, the Progressive Movement—a middle class rebellion against political and corporate corruption—was led by Presidents Theodore Roosevelt and Woodrow Wilson. During the Great Depression, President Franklin Delano Roosevelt's New Deal furthered the reform agenda and created a Democratic majority that dominated Congress until 1994. Throughout that entire period, the Republicans controlled the House of Representatives for only four years while the Democrats controlled it for fifty-eight years. During this time modern liberalism dominated government policy and the welfare state grew progressively larger.

It was not until William F. Buckley, Jr., who founded *National Review* magazine in 1955, that the tide began to slowly turn. *National Review* was a lonely voice of conservatism in an overwhelmingly liberal establishment. Then, in 1960, Senator Barry Goldwater wrote *Conscience of a Conservative,* a policy guidebook. This led to the Draft Goldwater movement in 1962, the nomination of Goldwater in 1964, and the seizing of power by the conservatives from the moderate establishment within the Republican Party. Then came Ronald Reagan.

In his speeches around the country for Goldwater, Ronald Reagan began many of his talks by saying, "I am going to speak of controversial things." The *New York Times* hated this and ridiculed the messenger. Reagan cheerfully persisted and the audiences grew in enthusiasm and size. People measured Reagan's values against the media's and decided Reagan was right. In 1966, he won the governorship of California in a landslide.

For the next fourteen years Governor Reagan toured the country talking about basic values, about changing Washington rather than managing it, about defeating the Soviet empire instead of seeking détente, and about cutting taxes instead of raising them. He understood "politics as history" and did not care about the petty day-to-day maneuverings of legislators and reporters. He was focused on building a tidal wave that would change the debate and create a new agenda.

When Ronald Reagan was sworn in as president in 1981, his commitment to change was an enormous shock to the elite media. They could accept a conservative campaigning on what they called red-meat issues, but the candidate was supposed to understand that when he won, he was supposed to drop the big ideas and return to politics as usual.

Instead President Reagan was committed to defeating the "Evil Empire," to having Gorbachev "tear down this wall," to cutting taxes and regulations, and to renewing the entrepreneurial spirit of America. All this stunned the elite media. The depth of President Reagan's commitment to his values and his persistence in advocating them can best be understood by reading Peter Schweizer's book *Reagan's War*. Schweizer noted that Reagan had concluded communism was evil in 1947. It was only thirty-five years later in 1982 that he was in a position to give his famous "Evil Empire" speech. President Reagan first called for tearing down the Berlin Wall in May 1967 in a televised debate with Robert Kennedy. Two decades later, in 1987, he came back as president and made his famous challenge. Two years later, the Berlin Wall was torn down by the German people.

By insisting on "politics as history," President Reagan achieved historic goals that virtually no one could have predicted in 1980. For our generation to be successful, we need a similar grassroots movement that demands profound change to defeat fundamental threats to our way of life. This movement has to be focused on values, on solutions, and on telling the truth even when it is controversial. The purpose of this book is to outline the case for such a movement, a 21st Century Contract with America.

The First Contract with America

The first Contract with America in 1994 was a remarkable tool for political and governmental change. Led by the Contract, the Republican Party had its biggest congressional victory since before the Great Depression. The results of November 1994 were not only stunning to most observers (almost none of whom expected a Republican majority even on election day), but was also a tidal wave of historic proportions. The Republican vote increased by nine million from 1990 to 1994 while the Democratic vote declined by a million. This swing of ten million votes between the two parties is the largest nonpresidential voter shift in American history. It had an impact on Senate elections, governorships, state legislative races, and every level of American politics.

What made the Contract truly revolutionary was that it had a governmental as well as political purpose. It was the only time in American history a federal legislative party—the House Republicans—adopted a contract instead of a platform. We bound ourselves to *do* something (a contract) and not simply to be *for* something (a platform). Because of the energy and spirit built around the Contract, the House Republicans (all but three actually signed the Contract) kept their word and voted on every single item in the first ninety-three days. The Contract accomplished:

1. The first major tax cut in sixteen years.
2. Real welfare reform, reducing the number of people on welfare by 60 percent and insisting that welfare recipients go to school or look for a job.
3. The first four consecutive balanced budgets since the 1920s, enabling our economy to enter a long period of very low interest rates with little risk of inflation.
4. The first financial audit of the House by an outside auditing firm in American history, a practice that continues today.
5. Term limits for committee chairmen in the House.
6. Applying to the House all the laws that apply to small business so politicians can learn what the self-employed and small business men and women endure from government.
7. Strengthening the military and intelligence capabilities of the United States.
8. The invention of the Thomas system that allows Internet access to the U.S. House of Representatives, bypassing lobbyists and privileged insiders.

The Contract was powerful because it outlined ideas that were championed by tenacious and determined leaders. It was Governor Reagan, for example, who began advocating welfare reform in 1970 at the National Governors' Conference. Congress passed welfare reform three times. President Bill Clinton vetoed it twice before he finally signed it in 1996—twenty-six years after President Reagan's remarks. Charles Murray, in his book *Losing Ground,* and Marvin Olasky, in his book *The Tragedy of American Compassion*, helped us win the argument about the need to replace a destructive system of dependency with a system of effort and opportunity. As Prime Minister Margaret Thatcher taught us, "first you have to win the argument and then you can win the vote."

The Contract was effective because it was based on the core values of the American people. We knew Americans valued work over welfare and believed that a balanced budget in peacetime is a moral imperative, even more than an economic one. We knew that Americans believed that the private sector was better at job and wealth creation than were government bureaucrats. We knew that Americans wanted the United States to be strong enough to defend itself in a dangerous world. What made us different from traditional Republican politicians was that, like President Reagan, we were prepared to boldly stand with the American people and ignore the editorial writers and liberal commentators who would predictably scoff at our "simplistic" (conservative) ideas.

We advocates of the Contract were also prepared to be "cheerfully persistent" in reaching out to the American people past the biases and the inadequacies of the news media. We used C-SPAN, talk radio, and emails. We gave speeches and visited local radio, television, and newspapers around the country (media outside the Beltway were often much more open to new ideas than the elite political press, which focused on insider political trivia). Our people-to-people efforts to communicate took years but we gradually built networks of activists who understood what we were doing and supported it enthusiastically.

The first Contract with America proved that it was possible to bring together people from all across America to forge a strong political majority that would keep its word and implement the program it campaigned on. If we have the same persistence and courage, we can win again. The first step is a new 21st Century Contract with America.

A 21st Century Contract with America

This is what needs to be done:

1. We must commit to a long war to defeat the terrorists and tyrants who would destroy America.
2. We must reestablish that our rights come from our Creator and that an America that has driven God out of the public arena is an America on the way to decay and defeat.
3. We must insist on patriotic immigration and patriotic education based on classic American history and the wisdom of the Founding Fathers and Abraham Lincoln.
4. We must transform our domestic institutions in order to harness modern science and technology to create jobs, wealth, and lead the world economy into the 21st century.
5. We must establish the opportunities for a personal Social Security account, a portable personal pension account, and a personal health savings account, so the wealth we create during our working lives is wealth we control.

The next chapters will discuss these five commitments and outline the practical steps all of us can take to meet this decade's challenges.

A 21st Century Contract with America

Key Provisions

We are committed to a safe, healthy, prosperous, and free America. We believe our children and grandchildren deserve the opportunities our parents and grandparents gave us.

In a rapidly changing world with new threats and new competitors, we must implement policies that will ensure America's leadership, safety, and prosperity. And we must reinvigorate the core values that have made America an exceptional civilization.

We do not believe the traditional instruments of government will reform themselves fast enough and thoroughly enough for the twenty-first century.

The entrenched lobbyists and entrenched bureaucracies will do all they can to minimize the changes no matter how vital those changes are to America's future. Self interest will dominate national interest if the normal political system operates with business as usual. The pressure of daily events will keep both the news media and most politicians focused on the immediate and the trivial rather than the long-term and the profoundly important.

Only a grassroots citizens' movement can insist on the level of change that is needed for our children and grandchildren to have a successful future.

Such a citizens' movement would have to be focused on goals rather than on interest groups. The goals define the America we want our children and grandchildren to have.

To achieve this future we will:

I

Defend America and our allies from those who would destroy us. To achieve security, we will develop the intelligence, diplomatic, information, defense, and homeland security systems and resources for success.

II

Transform the Social Security system into personal savings accounts that will enable every worker to have higher retirement incomes from their own work and avoid the need for financial support from their children.

III

Recenter America on the Creator from Whom all our liberties come. We will insist on a judiciary that understands the centrality of God in American history and reasserts the legitimacy of recognizing the Creator in public life.

IV

Establish patriotic education for our children and patriotic immigration for new Americans. To achieve this, we will renew our commitment to education about American citizenship based on American history and an understanding of the Founding Fathers and the core values of American civilization. We will insist that both our children and immigrants learn the key values and key facts of American history as the foundation of their growth as citizens.

V

Meet the triple economic challenges of an explosion in scientific and technological knowledge, an increasingly competitive world market, and the rise of China and India by implementing:

1 A new system of civil justice to reduce the burden of lawsuits and to incentivize young people to go into professions other than the law.
2 A dramatically simplified tax code that favors savings, entrepreneurship, investment, and constant modernization of equipment and technology.
3 Math and science learning equal to any in the world and educating enough young Americans to both discover the science of the future and to compete successfully in national security and the economy with other well-educated societies.
4 Investing in the scientific revolutions that are going to transform our world—particularly in energy, space, and the environment.
5 Transforming health care into a 21st Century Intelligent Health System that improves our health while lowering costs dramatically. In the process, American health care will become our highest value export and foreign exchange earning sector.

VI

Work to include every American in a system of patriotic stewardship so every person has a real opportunity to pursue happiness as their Creator endowed. Prepare for the aging of the baby boomers and their children so we can have active healthy aging with the best quality of life, the longest period of independent living, and the greatest prosperity. We will:

1 Develop a system in which those who wish to stay economically active are encouraged and incentivized to do so because active people live longer and healthier, have a greater opportunity to pursue happiness, and are less of a burden on their fellow citizens;
2 Develop a system of independent living and assisted living that increases the years in which people can be on their own and in most cases enables people to live their entire lives with freedom and dignity;
3 Develop a new model of quality long-term care in which both the care and the quality of life are compatible with a twenty-first century American expectation of progress and innovation;
4 Use the new technologies and new scientific knowledge to turn disabilities into capabilities and change government regulations and programs to help every American achieve the fullest possible ability to pursue happiness.

VII

Change the mindset of big government in Washington by replacing bureaucratic public administration with Entrepreneurial Public Management so government can operate with the speed, effectiveness, and efficiency of the information age.

VIII

Balance the federal budget and insist on a lean government, low tax, low interest rate economy to maximize growth in a competitive world.

IX

Insist on congressional reform to make the legislative branch responsive to the needs of the 21st century.

X

Ensure an election process that is honest, accountable, accurate, and free from the threat of illegal votes or subsequent litigation.

If we insist on these goals and insist on electing leaders at all levels dedicated to these goals, we will be able to leave our children and grandchildren an America of safety, health, prosperity, and freedom that would make our parents and grandparents proud. We too will have done our duty to our country and our achievements as citizens will be worthy of the America we inherited.

CHAPTER 1

WILL WE SURVIVE?

"IT IS THE ETERNAL STRUGGLE BETWEEN TWO PRINCIPLES, RIGHT AND WRONG, THROUGHOUT THE WORLD."

PRESIDENT ABRAHAM LINCOLN
DEBATE AT ALTON, ILLINOIS, OCTOBER 15, 1858

IMAGINE THE MORNING AFTER an attack even more devastating than 9/11. It could happen. The threats are real and could literally destroy our country.

There are weapons of mass destruction, weapons of mass murder, and weapons of mass disruption—nuclear is first, biological and chemical is second, electromagnetic pulse (EMP) is third. All are real, and we are lulled into complacency by the fact that none is currently being used. But if any of them were used, the effect could be catastrophic.

Despite spending billions of dollars on our national security, we are still unprepared. Our intelligence capabilities are—at most—one-third the size we need. Consider that the Federal Bureau of Investigation has hundreds of thousands of hours of terrorist intercepts that have not been heard, much less analyzed, because there are not enough translators. Our intelligence community has been studying

North Korea for nearly fifty years, yet we know almost nothing about the country. Our civilian national security bureaucracy is so weak, so slow, and so inefficient that only 5 percent of the $18 billion appropriated to help rebuild Iraq has been spent. Even our battle-proven military remains woefully unprepared for fighting the wars of the future.

America's lack of preparation, however, should not discourage us or even surprise us. Americans have had to rethink and reorganize for every major national security challenge in our history. We must recognize that we have three objectives to achieve.

First, we must defeat the radical wing of Islam as represented by al Qaeda and its affiliated terrorist groups, the Wahabbi sect, and terror-sponsoring Islamic states. Second, we must contain powers that could threaten us, including China, Russia, North Korea, Iran, and Pakistan—all of which have weapons of mass destruction. And finally, we must create a broad alliance of countries willing to defend peace and freedom.

As Ronald Reagan won the Cold War, so too can we win this war, as I'll show, by modeling and modifying President Reagan's strategy.

The Threat

The simple fact is: We have been warned. If anyone thinks terrorists don't threaten us, the question is: What would it take to convince you? If nearly 3,000 Americans dying on American soil in one day does not frighten you, what would?

The sobering reality is that terrorist leaders are determined to kill Americans and destroy our government and culture.

Consider the religious *fatwa* titled "A Treatise on the Legal Status of Using Weapons of Mass Destruction Against Infidels" that Osama bin Laden secured from Shaykh Nasir bin Hamd al-Fahd, a young and prominent Saudi cleric justifying the use of weapons of mass destruction (WMD) against Americans, in May 2003:

> Anyone who considers America's aggressions against Muslims and their lands during the past decades will conclude that striking her is permissible on the basis of the rule of treating one as one has been treated. No other argument need be mentioned. Some brothers have totaled the number of Muslims killed directly or indirectly by their weapons and come up with a figure of nearly ten million. . . . If a bomb that killed ten million of them and burned as much of their land as they have burned Muslim land was dropped on them, it would be permissible, with no need to mention any other argument. We might need other arguments if we wanted to annihilate more than this number of them.

Other al Qaeda leaders are equally explicit about killing many Americans. This statement is from Ayman Al-Zawahir: "We have not reached parity with them. We have the right to kill four million Americans—two million of them children—and to exile twice as many and wound and cripple hundreds of thousands. Furthermore, it is our right to fight them with chemical and biological weapons, so as to afflict them with the fatal maladies that have afflicted the Muslims because of the [Americans'] chemical and biological weapons."

The threat of mass deaths at times becomes a threat of extermination. As Hamas leader Abdel Aziz Rantisi stated in June 2003: "Not a single Jew will remain in Palestine."

In the *9/11 Commission Report*, the commissioners concluded: "Bin Laden and Islamist terrorists mean exactly what they say: To them America is the font of all evil, the "head of the snake, and it must be converted or destroyed."[1]

Americans cannot negotiate with al Qaeda. We have no common ground with terrorists. Al Qaeda and its affiliates can only be destroyed. We are in a war of survival—*and we could lose that war.* Our vulnerability is neither exaggerated nor a paranoid fantasy.

If these terrorists acquired nuclear weapons, they would use them against our cities. If they acquired biological weapons, they could kill millions. (One Nobel Prize winner told me that an engineered biological attack could kill 140 million Americans. Even a modest biological outbreak, like the 1918 flu pandemic, killed more people in one year than died in the four years of World War I.) And if the terrorists had chemical weapons, they could kill thousands.

Another threat can be from an electromagnetic pulse weapon—an explosion that could short-circuit our electrical systems. According to the commission of physicists assigned to study it, an EMP attack could collapse America into an 1860 world without electricity and reduce our advantage in military technology to zero. China and Russia have both considered limited nuclear attack options that, unlike their Cold War plans, employ EMP as the primary or sole means of attack. As recently as May 1999, during the NATO bombing of the former Yugoslavia, high-ranking members of the Russian Duma (Russia's parliament), meeting with a U.S. congressional delegation to discuss the Balkans conflict, raised the specter of a Russian EMP attack that would paralyze America.[2]

There are conventional threats too. Terrorists could launch a campaign of bombings and sniper attacks in the United States. The next time you watch a bombing in Israel, an attack in Russia, or violence in Iraq, know that it could happen here.

The Hart-Rudman Commission, a bipartisan commission that spent three years studying American security, warned in March 2001 that the primary threat to the United States was that within the next twenty-five years, a weapon of mass destruction—nuclear, chemical, or biological—could be used against American cities, probably from a terrorist attack. As early as September 1999, the commission warned: "States, terrorists, and other disaffected groups will acquire weapons of mass destruction and mass disruption, and some will use them. Americans will likely die on American soil, possibly in large numbers."[3]

The tragic and shocking events of 9/11 were actually of a much smaller scale than the dangers warned of by the Hart-Rudman Commission. The commission stated: "The greatest danger of another catastrophic attack in the United States will materialize if the world's most dangerous terrorists acquire the world's most dangerous weapons . . . al Qaeda has tried to acquire or make nuclear weapons for at least ten years . . . we mentioned officials worriedly discussing, in 1998, reports that Bin Laden's associates thought their leader was intent on carrying out a 'Hiroshima.' These ambitions continue."[4]

Thomas H. Kean, the chairman of the 9/11 Commission, said shortly after releasing the report: "Time is not on our side." Every day, terrorists try to acquire weapons of mass destruction and weapons of mass murder. Iran and North Korea continue to develop their nuclear and other weapons programs. There is constant danger of a coup by radical Islamists in nuclear-armed Pakistan.

And the greatest danger for us in meeting this threat is the weakness of our intelligence services. We do not have any significant intelligence on the enemy's plans, networks, and troop strength. We have not even been able to find Osama bin Laden.

Terrorism Is an Act of War

The Clinton administration consistently dealt with terrorism as a criminal matter. President George W. Bush recognized immediately that the 9/11 attack was an act of war and not the scene of a crime. He responded with military force—not detectives.

President Bush told us the truth: It will be a hard campaign, a long war, and we will suffer setbacks on occasion. "This war will not be like the war against Iraq a decade ago, with a decisive liberation of territory and a swift conclusion.... Our response involves far more than instant retaliation and isolated strikes. Americans should not expect one battle, but a lengthy campaign, unlike any other we have ever seen."[5]

Even after the initial military victory in Iraq, President Bush reiterated:

> We have difficult work to do in Iraq. We're bringing order to parts of that country that remain dangerous. We're pursuing and finding leaders of the old regime, who will be held to account for their crimes. We've begun the search for hidden chemical and biological weapons and already know of hundreds of sites that will be investigated. We're helping to rebuild Iraq, where the dictator built palaces for himself, instead of hospitals and schools. And we will stand with the new leaders of Iraq as they establish a government of, by, and for the Iraqi people.... The transition from dictatorship to democracy will take

time, but it is worth every effort. Our coalition will stay until our work is done. Then we will leave, and we will leave behind a free Iraq.[6]

Transformational wars always take time, and always mean overcoming setbacks: It took George Washington from 1776 to 1783 to win the Revolutionary War. It took Abraham Lincoln four years (1861 to 1864) to finally hit on a winning strategy to win the Civil War in 1865. And the Cold War lasted more than forty years.

We Must Know Our Enemies

To win the war we must know our enemy.

We have two immediate opponents, the irreconcilable wing of Islam and the rogue dictatorships that empower the radical Islamists. The irreconcilable wing of Islam considers America the great Satan. The Islamists cannot reconcile with a secular system of laws. They cannot tolerate a West that maintains a presence in the Arabian Gulf or that would defend Israel's right to survive as a country. They cannot tolerate freedom of speech, freedom of religion, or freedom for women. In short, their demands are irreconcilable with the modern world.

Politically correct secularists cannot understand that we are participants in a global civil war between the modernizing and irreconcilable wings of Islam. While the irreconcilable wing must be fought militarily, this is also a cultural, political, and economic war (as was the Cold War). This war is not primarily about terrorism, it is about an Islamist insurgency against the modern world.

A reasonable estimate would be that this war will last until 2070 (the Soviet Union lasted from 1917 to 1991, or seventy-four years).

An optimist could make a case for winning by 2025 or 2030. Alternatively this conflict could be a fact of life for several centuries (as the Catholic–Protestant wars were during the Reformation and Counter Reformation).

Because secular post-modern analysts refuse to take religion seriously, we describe "suicide bombers" while our opponents describe "martyrs." We see them as psychologically deranged where they see themselves as dedicated to God. We focus on body counts while our opponents see their dead as symbols for recruitment. We focus on weeks and months while our opponents patiently focus on decades and generations. We think of trouble spots while they think of global jihad. We are in a total mismatch of planning and understanding.

We are hunting down al Qaeda (a loose grouping of 3,000 to 5,000 people) while our opponents are vastly larger. As one counter-terrorism analyst suggested to me "about the time we wipe out al Qaeda there will be five to ten new organizations of equal or greater size." We can reasonably guess that about 3 to 4 percent of the 1.3 billion Muslims on the planet are potential terrorist recruits—a pool of 39 to 52 million young men. There might be more than 10,000 potential recruits for every current member of al Qaeda.

Virtually every expert believes the number of militants available to the Irreconcilables is growing much faster than we are killing them. We have no effective communication counter-strategy to the television stations like Al-Jazeera and Al-Arabiya that serve as multimillion (maybe multibillion) dollar force multipliers for the insurgency. Consider the tiny cost bin Laden pays for an audio tape that these stations broadcast to more than a third of the Arab world at no cost to al Qaeda.

The challenge of these potentially violent Irreconcilables is compounded by what George Tenet, former director of the Central Intelligence Agency, described as the Gray World.

The Gray World

Even small terrorist organizations can have global reach through the global criminal system of the Gray World: illegal narcotics and drug-dealing, illegal transportation across borders, international arms dealers, traditional international crime, and people smuggling.

Every year at least 800,000 slaves—mainly from Eastern Europe, Asia, and Africa—are smuggled into other countries, including democracies like Holland and the United States. About 90 percent of these slaves are women, many are children, and most are sold for sexual purposes. A system that can smuggle slaves can also smuggle terrorists.

This Gray World is made even more dangerous by the fact that it can produce income for the terrorist networks. The dramatic increase in heroin production in Afghanistan is a major threat to the pro-Western government in Kabul. In 2004, heroin producers were probably earning as much foreign currency as the Kharzai regime. It is likely over the next few years that Afghan heroin processors will increase their purchasing power and technological reach much faster than the bureaucracy in Kabul. Unchecked, this Gray World could become a major threat to the efforts to create a free, modern Afghanistan.

There is another complication arising from the Gray World. As international criminals of all types become wealthier and more sophisticated, they can corrupt law enforcement, politicians, and to some extent an entire society. As Mark Bowden illustrated in his book *Killing Pablo*—about the hunt for the billionaire cocaine lord Pablo Escobar in Medellin, Colombia—Escobar's wealth made him a local folk hero and bought him protection from the police. It took three years to track him down even though the Colombian and American governments knew he was somewhere in Medellin.

This Gray World has yet to be factored into our national security strategy. *What this means is that fighting international crime is synonymous with fighting our terrorist enemies.* A major part of our homeland defense buildup must be a large boost in the number of FBI and Border Patrol agents, as well as an enlargement of the Coast Guard. This and cooperation with international anti-criminal organizations like Interpol is vital to our war-winning strategy.

Ungoverned Areas and the Strategy of "No Sanctuaries"

In dealing with terrorists in the age of nuclear and biological weapons, we clearly have to assert a strategy of "no sanctuaries." It was this principle of "no sanctuaries" that led President George W. Bush to issue an ultimatum to the Taliban government of Afghanistan shortly after 9/11. It was the Taliban's refusal to end its sanctuary for bin Laden that led to the American liberation of Afghanistan. It is one thing to impose a "no sanctuary" rule on governments. It is quite another to try to eliminate sanctuaries in ungoverned areas of the world, such as we faced in Somalia in 1993. Today, our intelligence services know little about these areas of the world. Rapidly expanding our intelligence assets—native agents on the ground—as well as the number of special forces units that can swiftly be deployed for targeted covert strikes is crucial to winning this war.

Rogue Nations: Aiding and Abetting the Terrorists

The greatest threat of rogue dictatorships, like Iran or North Korea, is that they will sell weapons of mass destruction. While North

Korea—with nuclear, chemical, and biological weapons—is a big threat to South Korea and Japan, it is a very distant threat to the United States. But a North Korea willing to sell nuclear and biological weapons to terrorists is *very* dangerous to America. As Donald Macintyre reported in *Time* magazine: "The North Koreans certainly don't have a record of self-restraint. Ballistic missiles are its top foreign-exchange earner, according to U.S. government estimates. That trade pulls in between $150 million and $300 million a year—a tidy sum, given that the country's legitimate exports amount to about $600 million. No country sells more missiles; Egypt, Iran, Libya, Syria, Yemen, and possibly Iraq have all been customers."[7]

Before we toppled Saddam Hussein, Iraq presented a similar threat. We had every reason to believe Saddam Hussein would give or sell weapons of mass murder to a variety of terrorist groups. As has been well documented,[8] Saddam Hussein was closely tied to terrorists and had an interest in aiding them to attack the United States.

Another danger is that Pakistan might suffer an Islamist military coup and that Pakistan's nuclear weapons could be given to—or taken by—terrorists. The new Pakistani dictatorship could even announce that a weapon had been "stolen" and argue that it wasn't to blame if a bomb went off in the United States, Israel, India, or Europe.

The most dangerous country of all is Iran. Iran is the world's most aggressive terrorist sponsor. To quote analyst Rachel Ehrenfeld:

> Recent events have made it clear that the threat posed by Iran should be dealt with sooner rather than later. Today's 9/11 Commission report documents extensive ties between Iran and terrorism, and the mullahs' drive to create a nuclear weapon is well known. In recent days, Iranian officials and clerics have increased the incitement for violence against American and Coalition forces in Iraq. However, ending the real threat

this fundamentalist Islamic theocracy poses to the United States and the West may be impossible, thanks to the Left's and the pro-Islamists' non-stop assault on the president's credibility. The case against Iran should be air-tight. The Bush administration is now armed with: [1] The 9/11 Commission's report, documenting the logistical, operational and material support from Iran and Hezbollah (Iran's international terrorist arm) to al-Qaeda; [2] Iran's own admission of its intention to develop nuclear weapons; [3] Iran's increasing anti-American rhetoric; and [4] Iran's growing support of terrorism in Iraq. According to the just-released 9/11 Commission Report, Iran's support of al-Qaeda dates back to 1991, when operatives from both sides met in Sudan and agreed "to cooperate in providing support—even if only training—for actions carried out primarily against Israel and the United States." This is how the commission phrased it: "There is strong evidence that Iran facilitated the transit of al Qaeda members into and out of Afghanistan before 9/11, and that some of these were future 9/11 hijackers . . . however, *we cannot rule out the possibility of a remarkable coincidence . . .* [and] *we found no evidence that Iran or Hezbollah was aware of the planning for what later became the 9/11 attack.*"[9]

Iran is the most important foreign policy challenge for the president. It is central to the "web of terror" described by Lieutenant General Thomas McInerney (U.S. Air Force, retired) and Major General Paul Vallely (U.S. Army, retired) in their book *Endgame.*[10] But as Generals McInerney and Vallely also point out, we can change the regime in Iran by assisting the large number of Iranians who want to overthrow the Islamic dictatorship themselves. We must contain rogue nations, as we contained the communists, and where possible we must back groups—as Ronald Reagan backed the Contras in Nicaragua,

Solidarity in Poland, and the Afghans who fought the Soviets—who can help us "roll back" enemy regimes.

A Formula for Victory

It is clear that we will need a strong homeland security system for generations to come. We can, however, achieve a dramatically safer world than we have today. President George W. Bush has made a good beginning by outlining the *only* strategy that can make America secure: "If the Middle East grows in democracy, prosperity, and hope, the terrorist movement will lose its sponsors, lose its recruits, and lose the festering grievances that keep terrorists in business."[11] And again: ". . . we are extending the peace by supporting the rise of democracy, and the hope and progress that democracy brings, as the alternative to hatred and terror in the broader Middle East. In democratic and successful societies, men and women do not swear allegiance to malcontents and murderers; they turn their hearts and labor to building better lives. And democratic governments do not shelter terrorist camps or attack their neighbors. When justice and democracy advance, so does the hope of lasting peace."[12]

Because we are involved in a civil war within Islam, we must work to turn the Islamic world against the Irreconcilables. Just as the Cold War was fought in part as a propaganda war pitting the appeal of democracy against communism, so too we need the Peace Corps and other government agencies to sponsor pro-Western secular schools and charities throughout the Islamic world. Most important, we need big broadcast networks that communicate to the Islamic world Western ideas about the rule of law, private property, and freedom. We need to broadcast our civic culture so that the Arab world gets a different view of the West than what it gets from Al Jazeera and Michael Moore.

Should We Be on Offense, or Is That Provocative?

In 1941, President Franklin Delano Roosevelt authorized U.S. warships to seek out German submarines operating in the western Atlantic and sink them. He said: "When you see a rattlesnake poised to strike, you do not wait until he has struck to crush him."

For many people on the American and international Left, there is almost no provocation that would justify an aggressive American military effort overseas. If Hitler was not evil enough to justify war in some people's minds, we should not be surprised that coexistence with Saddam Hussein or Kim Jong Il strikes them as reasonable.

For everyone else, the practical question is simple: How do we best protect America? President George W. Bush has rightly taken the position that we have ample proof of who our enemies are and we should prevent their attacks and pre-empt their plans.

Can we rely on our historic allies to support us? In particular, will France—the leader of the European Union—support us?

The Left says that with better diplomacy, we could have France by our side in Iraq. But this ignores France's long history of making profits from the regime of Saddam Hussein.

French President Jacques Chirac pushed very hard for French economic interests in Iraq, even when Iraq was under United Nations sanctions. Banque Nationale de Paris-Paribas was the sole bank administering the $64 billion United Nations "Oil for Food" program without public accounting or scrutiny. The "Oil for Food" scandal (in which at least $21.3 billion was estimated stolen from the Iraqi people) implicates a number of French business figures. Selfishness and a narrow, petty definition of national self-interest seem to be the hallmark of French policies in the Middle East.

If France cannot be counted on, many on the Left believe we should rely on the United Nations and other international organizations. These, they believe, are a substitute for American power and American endurance. But they are wrong.

Why Not Rely on the United Nations and the World Court?

The World Court today is chaired by a Chinese judge whose country is a totalitarian society repressively occupying Tibet, refusing to hold open elections in Hong Kong, and threatening to invade Taiwan. In 2003, Libya, which was ruled by the dictator Muammar Qadhafi, became chairman of the Human Rights Commission. In 2004, the United Nations included Sudan on the Human Rights Commission even though its Islamist dictatorship is accused of murdering thousands of Africans, fostering a starvation policy that could kill a million more Africans this year, and that has been responsible for what Secretary General Kofi Annan says is the biggest humanitarian crisis on the planet.

The first time the United Nations facilities in Iraq were bombed, the United Nations simply fled the country and gave up its responsibilities. The U.N. was impotent in East Timor in the face of massacres of Christian Timorese by the Indonesians. It was the Australian Army that unilaterally established order and protected innocent people from being massacred. There is no evidence that the U.N. has been successful in creating safety for people except when the major powers intervened. Either the United States leads or the hard things do not get done.

France and the United Nations did not defeat communism, the United States did. For the foreseeable future, the center of effective power in the world is going to be America. This is simply a fact of life that must be reflected in our budgets for defense, intelligence, and homeland security.

The Problem with Our Intelligence System

The failure to find stockpiles of weapons of mass destruction in Iraq has led to a remarkably one-sided assault on the intelligence community. Our intelligence in Iraq was apparently wrong—and so was the intelligence of every other Western country—and overestimated Saddam Hussein's capabilities to produce weapons of mass destruction. But it is also true that in 1991, the intelligence community dramatically *underestimated* how dangerous Saddam was: Intelligence experts were shocked by how advanced Iraqi nuclear[13] and biological programs were (and Saddam Hussein had already used chemical weapons).

The Clinton administration and the Democrats consistently cut the intelligence budget. They drastically restricted the use of human intelligence. They had a strong bias against spending on intelligence and national security. As the 9/11 Commission noted: "Cuts in national security expenditures at the end of the Cold War led to budget cuts in the national foreign intelligence program from fiscal years 1990 to 1996 and essentially flat budgets from fiscal years 1996 to 2000 (except for the so-called Gingrich supplemental to the fiscal year 1999 budget and two later, smaller supplementals). These cuts compounded the difficulties of the intelligence agencies."[14] Moreover, the report notes, national security spending was treated not as an investment, but as a mere expense: "Apart from the Gingrich supplemental . . . the key decisions on overall allocation of resources for national security issues in the decade before 9/11—including counterterrorism funding—were made in the president's Office of Management and Budget."[15]

Those of us who were fighting for more resources for intelligence and for a more effective program of human intelligence watched with dismay as the Left cut funding, crippled the gathering of intelligence with legal restrictions, and treated counter-terrorism funding as inconsequential. The liberals in Congress who now attack the intelligence community did the most to weaken it.

Intelligence is difficult work and in an age of weapons of mass murder and mass destruction, it is extraordinarily important work. We need a bigger intelligence system with more robust capabilities. This means a long-term strategy to set up many intelligence agents working in many different countries. It will require much bigger budgets and much more support than the Left has been willing to provide. To achieve all the intelligence coverage we want will require an intelligence community about three times the size of the current system.

Why Iraq Has Been Harder Than We Expected

While the Iraq War was just and the military campaign brilliant, the process of creating a democratic Iraq has been difficult. The decision to have an American administration in Baghdad was a mistake. We seemed to be doing relatively well in Iraq until late May 2003 when the Coalition Provisional Authority (CPA) transitioned into power.

Instead of the CPA, we should have created an interim Iraqi government in June 2003 as we had in Afghanistan. It took only three weeks to identify Hamid Kharzai in Afghanistan. The people actually involved in Iraq's interim government in June 2004 were all known and available in 2003.

We also underestimated the effect of the Arab media's propaganda campaign against us. We had no information program in the Arab world or in Europe capable of effectively communicating what we were trying to do. CPA media efforts were wrongly focused on American public opinion, not Iraqi public opinion. That made it much harder for us to mobilize Iraqis to our side.

In the Second World War, General Dwight Eisenhower understood that getting along with British Prime Minister Winston Churchill and creating public support for an Anglo-American coalition was central to victory. In 1942, while in London, he spent every Tuesday at lunch and every Friday evening at dinner with Churchill building the mutual understanding that was central to fighting the war.

At a different level, General George Marshall recruited Frank Capra—an Academy Award–winning director (whose career included *Mr. Smith Goes to Washington*)—to make the *Why We Fight* series of films. General Marshall thought these films were so important that he personally oversaw their development. It is notable that two of these films, *Battle of Russia* and *Desert Victory*, were specifically designed to enhance relations with our Allies.

From 1947 to 1952, the United States used the Marshall Plan, covert support of anti-communists, and other means to prevent Greece,

Turkey, Italy, and France from falling to the communists. Throughout the Cold War, the United States carried on robust anti-communist propaganda efforts that included the Voice of America and Radio Liberty.

In the global struggles against fascism and communism, the United States waged a military, economic, and propaganda war. Yet we have done nothing similarly organized and coherent in the war against Islamists and the rogue states.

And there have been other mistakes.

The decision of the CPA to disband the Iraqi military, putting hundreds of thousands of armed young men out of work, was a disaster that our military warned against. Had the Iraqi army been kept intact—as General Tommy Franks and General Michael DeLong recommended[16]—it is possible that most of the subsequent violence would have been averted.

The CPA also delayed the American military in training the new Iraqi army. We needed to move Iraqis front and center as rapidly as possible and we simply failed to do so. We needed a military in Iraq that spoke, looked, and worshiped like other Iraqis in order to gain intelligence and win the propaganda battle in Iraq.

Another obstacle was that Saddam had run down the economy much more than we expected, so the process of recovery became a process of rebuilding an exhausted infrastructure. Moreover, Saddam had destroyed much of Iraqi civil society, and the remnants of Saddam's Sunni-Baathist power structure were better organized and had access to many more weapons than we anticipated (the massive scale of Saddam's armories around Iraq was a surprise even to the analysts who had been looking at pictures of them).

When visiting China in August 2004, I was briefed by Chinese Communist Party experts on their long relationship with the Iraqi

Baathist Party. They believed that the Baathist Party had cohesion even without Saddam. As an organized political party themselves, the Chinese communists had a real appreciation for the staying power of a party developed along fascist-communist lines. I know of no American intelligence that predicted the level of Baathist cohesion and willingness to fight that we encountered. I also know of no effort on our part to ask the Russians and Chinese about their understanding of the Baathists. The failure of our political analysis led to the failure of our postwar policing in Iraq for which we were unprepared and for which we still lack adequate intelligence.

Along with weak intelligence on the Baathist Party and the anti-American insurgent forces, we lacked a strategy for dealing with insurgents and terrorists once we had captured them. This lack of strategic planning led to the tragedy of the Abu Ghraib prison scandal.

In late June 2004, the Coalition Provisional Authority finally turned power over to an Iraqi interim government, and the new American ambassador, John Negroponte, has done a fine job. He has stayed off television and focused instead on helping the Iraqis solve their own problems.

And we should be clear: There are a lot of problems. Iraq is a mess. It is going to remain a mess for a long time. We are trying to help a brutalized people. They have a bankrupt infrastructure. They have a shattered civil society. They have no experience in self-government. We are trying to help the Iraqis create a prosperous, democratic future. And we are trying to do all this while fighting an army of insurgents. We have consistently underestimated how hard rebuilding Iraq will be and how long the job will take. I have seen no evidence that we know how to defeat the insurgents who fight in Iraq. We still lack the necessary intelligence, communications efforts, and Iraqi military and police units to beat the insurgents.

The danger in Afghanistan and Iraq is a reversion to civil war and despotism. We need to understand that both Iraq and Afghanistan will take years to win if we define victory as a stable government that brings safety, health, prosperity, and freedom to its people. But if we have patience and determination, we can almost certainly help these two countries achieve a decent future and make them democratic models for the Islamic world.

How to Win

As President George W. Bush said in his Statement on National Security Strategy in September 2002, "The major institutions of American national security were designed in a different era to meet different requirements. All of them must be transformed." He is absolutely right. To win the wars of the twenty-first century we need transformational change in the way we think about national security.

We must ensure the United States has:

- *The best intelligence capabilities in the world to prevent and preempt terrorism.* We need to triple the size of our intelligence agencies. We need more analysts who are linguists; we need analysts with a better grasp of history and politics; and we need students of religion and culture. We need an intelligence community in which dissent is honored and respected and decision makers are given a range of views, not groupthink. And we need to dramatically increase the number of agents in the field and the number of covert operations forces.
- *The best system to capitalize on new breakthroughs in militarily applicable science and technology.* We need to keep our technological

edge with "smart" bombs and more sophisticated weapons and intelligence. We also need to use real-time information age technology to meet the rhythm of post-war rebuilding. As General David Petraeus, who is responsible for training, mentoring, and equipping the new Iraqi army, said: "Money is to reconstruction what ammunition is to a military battle." Ronald Reagan used technology to end the Cold War with his Star Wars program. We need to use technology in a way that will compel our current enemies to surrender.

- *An effective message and communications system to win the propaganda war.* We need to overmatch the propaganda of Al Jazeera and other media outlets hostile to the United States with a hugely upgraded effort of Arabic and Farsi language radio and television broadcasts to the Middle East twenty-four hours a day. We must also ask our diplomats to aggressively advance American policy, American values, the principles of democratic capitalism, and the advantages that come with a free, tolerant, and open society. Like our military men and women on the front lines, our diplomats must take risks in arguing for America. In the War on Terror, quiet diplomacy is no longer enough. As an example of transformation in American diplomatic policy, we need a new approach to the Israeli-Palestinian conflict to win the war against terrorism on behalf of both the Israeli and Palestinian people. For more on this topic, go to www.newt.org.
- *A homeland security system that can deal with any threat.* The creation of the Department of Homeland Security was a reorganization of existing government red tape, markedly bureaucratic infighting, and congressional pork barrel spending rather than a transformational change in the way we protect the United States.

To be effective the Department of Homeland Security needs to be prepared to cope with any threat—nuclear, biological, chemical, and conventional—that might hit our homeland. That means dramatically enlarging the FBI, the Coast Guard, the Border Patrol, and our emergency response capabilities.

- *A military shaped for twenty-first century challenges.* As Army Chief of Staff Peter Shoomacher has begun, we need to reorganize our regular army into quickly deployable expeditionary forces. We should build on President George W. Bush's efforts to change our Cold War military basing structure, closing many European bases and using the savings to set up forward operating bases in Central Asia, South Asia, and the Middle East.[17] We will continue to need a rapidly deployable Air Force, Navy, and Marine Corps of a size capable of fighting a two or even three theater war. After the Cold War, we drastically reduced the size of our military as a "peace dividend." But today we are in another long struggle and we need to build up our military, as Ronald Reagan did in the 1980s.
- *A successful foreign policy requires making the right decision, communicating the right decision, and implementing the right decision.* Unfortunately, in Washington we often exhaust ourselves merely getting to the right decision. We forget the second and third steps.

Simultaneously leading the world, defeating the Irreconcilable Islamists, forcing rogue dictatorships into acceptable behavior (or replacing them), building up our intelligence and military capabilities to cope with China and Russia and other threats, making the necessary transformations in our foreign policy bureaucracy, and securing our homeland will be an enormous undertaking.

But this challenge is no greater than winning the Revolutionary War against the most powerful nation on earth, winning the Civil War to keep the Union together, organizing a global war to defeat Nazi Germany and Imperial Japan, or sustaining a Cold War for forty-five years until the Soviet Empire collapsed.

We have risen to the challenge before and we can do so again.

For more information on national security, visit **www.newt.org/winningthefuture**

Chapter 2

Social Security Prosperity

Social Security is still considered untouchable by many politicians who think to go near it is political death. But the financial rewards for every American from Social Security reform and the creation of personal investment accounts are so great that Social Security reform should be a litmus test for your congressional vote. An average income couple in America, empowered to invest in personal accounts throughout their careers, each start out earning $20,000 a year or less. By age forty, the husband is earning $40,000 and the wife is earning $30,000. At retirement they will accumulate $829,800 if we create personal investment accounts—enough to pay them double what Social Security promises them, but cannot pay.[1]

Given the rewards that personal investment accounts offer to working Americans, it is not surprising that for over a decade, polls have shown that a large majority support such an option.[2] A Zogby International poll found that 68 percent of respondents would support "changing the system to give younger workers the chance to invest a portion of their Social Security taxes through individual accounts similar to IRAs or 401(k)s." Hispanics supported such an option by 72 percent, union households by 64 percent, and African Americans by 58 percent.

A 1999 *USA Today* poll found the public strongly opposed every major change to Social Security except one, a personal investment account option, which was favored by 66 percent of respondents. In 1997, Mark Penn conducted a poll for President Clinton that found that 73 percent of *Democrats* favored a personal account option for at least part of the program. These poll results have been borne out in recent elections. President Bush campaigned openly in 2000 on a personal account option for Social Security. He won while actually taking a majority of the senior vote in Florida. He campaigned even more aggressively on the idea in 2004, and won with an even bigger margin.

Leading Democratic opponents of personal accounts said the 2002 mid-term elections would be a referendum on such reform. Republican candidates who had supported the idea were bitterly attacked by the Democrats. The Democratic National Committee web site featured a cartoon video showing President Bush pushing seniors in wheelchairs off a cliff. Yet these Republican candidates won race after race, including many contested and high-profile races. Indeed, not one candidate seems to have been defeated on the issue. As political handicapper John Zogby reported after the election, "In every race where Social Security was a major issue, the pro-account candidate won."[3]

Now voices from the other side of the spectrum are beginning to turn towards such reform as well. At a December 3, 2002, Democratic Leadership Council Conference at New York University, former President Bill Clinton said the following:

> If you don't like privatizing Social Security, and I don't like it very much, but you want to do something to try to increase the rate of return, what are your options? Well one thing you could do is to give people one or two percent of the payroll tax, with the same options

> that Federal employees have with their retirement accounts, where you have three mutual funds that almost always perform as well or better than the market and a fourth option to buy government bonds, so you get the guaranteed Social Security return and a hundred percent safety just like you have with Social Security.[4]

Indeed, it has long since been forgotten that a plurality of the Social Security Advisory Committee that Clinton appointed in 1995 advocated a personal account option for Social Security that would allow workers to shift 5 percent of their payroll tax to the accounts. That should be the minimum for any new proposal.

In December 2002, the *Washington Post* followed Clinton's comments with an editorial that said the following:

> It makes sense to consider the merits of a pension system in which at least a part of the money that ordinary workers pay into Social Security is invested in the private sector. The return on capital investment is higher, historically, than the growth in wage levels that support the payroll tax. Even in the 1930s, a privately invested system, had it existed, would have been able to distribute higher benefits than the present structure. It should not be taboo to discuss a system that might provide the poor, in particular, with higher benefits in old age, and that would encourage saving in a country that is notoriously bad at it.[5]

Even though there is strong, broad, public support for the idea of personal accounts, it does not mean enacting a personal account option into law will be easy. The Left has a simple, Manichean view of the world—government good, private markets bad—and they will fight against the idea with a religious fervor.

Furthermore, don't expect opponents to fight against the idea with any intellectual honesty. Vulnerable seniors will be frightened and milked for political donations with ridiculous claims that this or that candidate will take away their Social Security, their homes, and the food on their table. In the past, there were campaigns that sent workers into nursing homes to tell extremely frail residents that the Republican candidate would throw them out of the home and onto the snow if they did not sign an absentee ballot for the Democrat opponent.

The Basic Structure of Social Security

Social Security is the single largest federal program and bigger than the entire budget of most countries. For fiscal year 2005, the Social Security payroll tax is projected to raise $575 billion, or 28 percent of total federal taxes for the year. Social Security expenditures are projected to be $515 billion, or 21.5 percent of total federal spending.

We spend more on Social Security than on national defense, even in a time of war. National defense spending in 2005 is projected to be $451 billion, 12 percent less than Social Security expenditures. For fiscal 2006, defense expenditures are projected to be 18 percent less than Social Security spending.

Social Security was enacted in 1935 as a central component of Franklin Roosevelt's New Deal. It was financed by a new payroll tax of 1 percent on both employer and employee, assessed on the first $3,000 of wage income each year. This resulted in a maximum annual tax of $60 for each worker, which stayed at that level until 1950, when it was raised to $90. In return for the tax, the program paid benefits to retirees after they reached age sixty-five.

As early as the mid–1970s, actuaries began predicting that tax revenues would eventually be insufficient to pay promised benefits. Congress responded in 1977 by passing amendments designed to "fix" the problem. President Jimmy Carter proclaimed that they would ensure the solvency of Social Security "for the rest of this century and well into the next one." But just a few years later, in 1981, the program's actuaries were back again projecting that the program would run short of funds within a few years.

President Reagan's budget director David Stockman developed a plan to close the gap for a while by reducing the rate of growth of Social Security benefits. Before the administration could even formally propose the plan, the Senate voted 96–0 on a resolution asking the president not to even send the proposals to Capitol Hill. This led to the formation of a bipartisan commission chaired by Federal Reserve chairman Alan Greenspan.

Through the commission, the administration negotiated a final package that for the first time relied more on restraining benefits than on raising taxes. The 1983 amendments kept Social Security paying the bills, but the actuaries continued to project an enormous, never-ending financial gap. The latest annual report of the Social Security Board of Trustees projects that Social Security will run short of funds to pay promised benefits in 2042.[6] Workers born in 1975 can expect to be retiring that year.

There is one basic feature in the structure of Social Security that is central to all of its problems and key to understanding the real solution: Social Security operates on a pay-as-you-go basis. This means the taxes of today's workers are not saved and invested to finance their future benefits but are paid out to finance the benefits of today's retirees. The future benefits of today's workers will be paid out of the future taxes of those who are working at the time. Social Security as structured today is a redistribution system, not a savings and investment system.

Even the current short-term annual surpluses are not saved and invested. Those funds are lent to the federal government in return for IOUs held in the Social Security Trust Fund. The government then spends that money on everything from welfare to State Department embassies. For example, about 90 percent of the current Social Security tax revenues of $575 billion will be spent this year on Social Security benefits of $515 billion. This means $60 billion will be lent to the federal government for more Social Security Trust Fund IOUs and spent on the rest of the federal government's $2.4 trillion budget.

Social Security's Long-Term Financing Crisis

A poll in the early 1990s found that more than twice as many young adults believed in UFOs as believed Social Security would still exist by the time they retire. Those young adults were on to something. Continuing to pay all promised benefits would require a massive rise in the total payroll tax rate from 12.4 percent today to about 18 percent—a 50 percent increase.[7] Moreover, the tax would have to be raised every year thereafter as the cost of full benefits as a percent of taxable payroll continues on a permanent climb. The projection stops in 2080 when the payroll tax rate would have to be close to 20 percent to pay all promised benefits. Then the increase would have to continue indefinitely after this as well.

In fact, the true financial crisis starts much sooner than 2042. In year 2018, the system will begin to run a deficit. In order to keep paying benefits, the trust fund will have to start turning in the IOUs it has been accumulating to get extra cash from the federal government. To get that cash, the government will have to raise taxes, cut other spending, or increase its deficits and borrow. From 2018 until the trust funds run out in 2042, the federal government will have to come up with an additional $8 trillion in today's dollars for Social Security in order to keep paying all promised benefits during that period. That is a huge financial crisis, starting just thirteen years from now.

If Social Security were a fully funded savings and investment system, then enough reserve assets would be on hand to pay all the future benefits that had been earned at any point.[8] By contrast, in the current pay-as-you-go system, we must continue to bring new workers into the economy and tax them at higher and higher levels in order to fund the growing number of retirees.

Most people know that the large baby boom population is one reason for the potential crisis. Birth rates soared soon after the soldiers returned home from World War II and remained at a high level until the early 1960s. Those born during this period will begin retiring in hordes less than ten years from now, causing Social Security benefit obligations to soar.

But that's only half the story. The baby boom was followed by a baby bust. The development of the birth control pill, the legalization of abortion, and changing social attitudes led to a sharp decline of birth rates starting in the early 1960s. This occurred not only in the United States, but in all Western countries, much more so, in fact, in Western Europe.

The U.S. fertility rate declined from 3.8 in 1957, to 2.43 in 1970, to 1.77 in 1975.[9] The fertility rate needs to be at least 2.1 to maintain a stable indigenous population. But the U.S. rate stayed well below this level until 1990, when it climbed back up, around 2.1, where it has stayed since that time.

What this means is that just as the baby boom generation retires, the generation of workers behind them will be experiencing much slower growth. This is a disaster for a pay-as-you-go system like Social Security. Just when benefit obligations will be soaring due to the retirement of the baby boom generation, the growth of taxes paid by the baby bust generation of workers behind them will be slowing down. Population increases due to immigration make America better off than Europe or Japan, but nonetheless there will be considerable financial pressure on the children and grandchildren of the baby boomers if we stay with the current static model of income transfers between generations.

Another major factor causing the long term Social Security financing crisis is increasing life expectancy. The baby boom generation is not only large, but it is expected to live much longer than previous generations, resulting in greater benefit obligations for Social Security.

In 1940, when Social Security was starting, life expectancy was 61.4 years for men and 65.7 for women.[10] Social Security's promise to pay full benefits, starting at age 65, was actually a promise to pay those benefits to less than half the population.

But today, life expectancy is about 74.4 for men and 79.5 for women.[11] By the time those entering the work force today start retiring, Social Security's actuaries project that life expectancy will have increased to 79.2 for men and 83.3 for women.[12] And that projection is based on a decline in the rate of increase in life expectancy we have experienced since 1940. More likely, with the high-tech medicines of the twenty-first century, life expectancy will increase faster, not slower, than in the last half of the twentieth century.

These are the reasons why the number of workers paying taxes to Social Security has declined from 4.2 in 1945 to 3.3 today per retiree.[13] It is projected to fall to 2.0 workers per retiree by 2040.[14] The prospect of longer lives for Americans would turn from a great joy to a great burden and could even lead to intergenerational bitterness.

Consider Europe's present pension crisis. Virtually every European government will continue to face huge budget deficits as the number of people receiving retirement pensions increases while the number of people still working and paying taxes stagnates and declines. Reforming Social Security with personal accounts would save us from a similar fate.

We Can Do Better

But there is an even bigger problem for Social Security than its long-term financing crisis. The program is no longer a good deal for working people today. Even if the program could pay all its promised benefits, the benefits would still represent a low, below-market return on the huge taxes workers and their employers now pay into the program. If today's workers could save and invest instead in their own personal accounts, they would likely receive far higher returns and benefits than Social Security now promises them, let alone what it can pay. With a long investment time frame, the risk of investing in the financial markets is significantly reduced.

The long-term real rate of return on corporate stocks is at least 7.0 to 7.5 percent.[15] In fact, going all the way back to 1926, when the most reliable data starts, the real rate of return on large company stocks listed on the New York Stock Exchange has been 7.5 percent.[16] The real return on smaller company stocks on the Exchange has been even higher, at 9.2 percent.[17] This period covers the Great Depression, World War II, more intermediate-size wars, the turbulent inflation/recession years of the 1970s, and the recent high-tech bubble collapse. The long term real return on corporate bonds has been around 3.5 percent.[18] At these rates, a portfolio of half stocks and half bonds over a worker's career would earn a net annual real return of 5 percent. A portfolio of two-thirds stocks and one-third bonds over a working career would earn a net real return of 5.75 percent.[19]

By contrast, Peter Ferrara and Michael Tanner, in a Cato Institute study, calculated that for most workers—middle aged and younger—the real rate of return on the taxes they and their employers pay into Social Security would be 1 to 1.5 percent or less.[20] For many it would be zero or negative.

One example in the Ferrara and Tanner study calculated the real rate of return promised by Social Security for a two-earner average income couple. The husband earned the average income for males each year and the wife earned the average income for females. Again, assume Social Security somehow is able to pay all of its promised benefits. The real rate of return this couple would receive on the taxes paid by them and their employers would be less than 1 percent—0.78 percent. For an average-income single worker, the real return would be even less, 0.31 percent. A widely noted Heritage Foundation study[21] found quite similar results, as have others.

But the outlook is even worse, since we know that Social Security will not be able to magically pay all of its promised benefits. Under the current system, either taxes will have to be increased by more than 50 percent, or benefits will have to be cut by 40 percent or more, or some combination of the two. This would dramatically lower the returns discussed above. Most workers would then expect a zero or even negative real rate of return. In other words, instead of getting a return on your savings, you are currently transferring your savings as taxes for a payout that may be less in benefits than what you and your employers paid in over your career—a negative rate of return. No one would find that acceptable when investing in the stock or bond market.

This large difference in returns adds up to an enormous difference in accumulated assets and benefits over a lifetime of work, investment, and retirement. Take the case of an average two-income couple noted at the outset. Suppose they could invest in a personal account over their entire careers equivalent to the account proposed in the Ryan–Sununu bill discussed later in this chapter. With two-thirds invested in stocks and one-third invested in bonds, and earning standard market returns, they would reach retirement with almost $1 million in today's dollars. That would be enough to pay them twice what Social Security promises but cannot pay.[22]

Why this enormous gulf between the payouts of personal accounts and Social Security? Unlike Social Security, the personal accounts operate as a fully funded savings and investment system. The money paid in is saved and invested in America's companies through the financial markets. These capital investments increase production, which provides more resources to pay workers higher benefits.

African Americans Get the Worst Deal in Social Security

The poor deal offered by Social Security applies with a vengeance to African Americans because they have much shorter life expectancies than the general population. Consequently, they have fewer retirement years to collect benefits. A black male born today has a life expectancy of 65.8 years, while the Social Security retirement age by the time he retires is age sixty-seven.[23] This means African Americans on average receive even lower returns on the taxes they pay into the system. The Heritage Foundation study calculated that a single black male born in 1970 could expect a real return from Social Security of −1.5 percent, even if all promised Social Security benefits were somehow paid.[24] The return for an average-income two-earner family with children is effectively 0 percent.[25]

With personal accounts, workers who die before retirement or just after retirement would be able to leave the funds to their children or other heirs. Moreover, social organizations like the National Association for the Advancement of Colored People (NAACP) could offer annuities promising a monthly benefit for life focused exclusively on their African American membership. Those annuities could then take into account the lower life expectancies of African Americans and pay higher retirement benefits. If one group has the most to gain from personal social security accounts, it is African Americans.

Hispanics and Social Security

Hispanics also suffer from a special problem under Social Security. The Hispanic population is much younger than the general population, and since the return paid by Social Security is falling over time, younger populations get lower returns on average than others. Only 5 percent of Hispanic Americans are over sixty-five, compared to

12 percent of the general population.[26] Moreover, only about 30 percent of Hispanic Americans over sixty-five receive any retirement income from assets, compared to 68 percent of the general population.[27] Clearly, Hispanic Americans are among those who would also have a lot to gain from a personal account option for Social Security.

Married Working Women and Social Security

Working women would get a much better deal with personal accounts. A working woman is entitled to retirement and survivor benefits under Social Security based on the taxes her husband and his employers paid. If she works, she gets the benefits only if they are higher than her own projected Social Security benefits. She gets no additional benefits for all her years working and paying into the system. If, however, her own Social Security retirement benefits are higher than her husband's record, then she gets those benefits but loses the benefits she would otherwise be entitled to from her husband. With personal accounts, by contrast, both husband and wife retain control over all the investments and savings they have paid.

Social Security and the Economy

About thirty years ago, Harvard economics professor Martin Feldstein, chairman of the National Bureau of Economic Research, began writing about the effects of the rapidly growing Social Security system on the economy. His conclusion was that Social Security was becoming a major drag on the economy.

Feldstein found that because workers assume Social Security will pay for their retirement, they don't save for it, or sharply reduce what they would otherwise save. Since Social Security operates as a pay-as-you-go system, with no real savings, the result is a net loss of actual savings and investment. With the Social Security taxes that finance retirement benefits currently running at about $575 billion a year, or about one-fourth of total annual private savings, the net loss is huge.

Feldstein buttressed his analysis with substantial econometric work concluding that Social Security reduces national saving by 40 percent or more. Studies by others have varied from finding similar results to results only about half as large. But even at the lower estimates, the loss of savings and investment would reduce America's gross domestic product (GDP) by about 5 percent each year. At Feldstein's original estimates the loss of GDP would be about 10 percent a year. With GDP currently running about $11 trillion a year, we are talking about losses in the range of $500 billion to a trillion dollars a year.

But there is still more. The payroll tax sharply reduces the net wages workers receive for working. The loss of savings and investment means lower productivity and so less wages as well. This reduces the labor supply and causes other distortions in the labor markets. Feldstein estimates that the result is another loss of GDP of 1 percent a year.[28]

Modernizing Social Security through personal accounts would raise take-home pay and free workers to put hundreds of billions and ultimately trillions of dollars in savings and investment; that would be a huge benefit to our economy. The accounts indeed represent a new, very large tax-free shelter for saving and investment. It would be the equal of a capital gains tax cut to further stimulate the economy. All of this adds up to a dramatic increase in savings and investment—and an economic boom.[29]

The Ryan–Sununu Bill

Is all this a pipe dream? Something that can never happen politically? No.

Last summer, Representative Paul Ryan and Senator John Sununu introduced a bill in the House and the Senate that provides for a personal account option for Social Security and solves the long-term problems of the program. The bill offers one of the most sweeping, fundamental reforms in our nation's history. For the major components of the bill, visit www.newt.org/winningthefuture.[30]

The bill has been officially scored by the chief actuary of Social Security to determine its impact on Social Security and federal finances.[31] The chief actuary reported that under the reform plan, "the Social Security program would be expected to be solvent and to meet its benefit obligations throughout the long-range period 2003 through 2077 and beyond."[32] The reform eliminates completely the unfunded liability of Social Security, currently officially estimated at $11 trillion. This is effectively the largest reduction in government debt in world history. Moreover, the Ryan–Sununu reform plan would actually cut taxes and increase benefits over time.

The reform plan starts producing surpluses by 2030. Those surpluses are first devoted to paying off the debt issued in the earlier years of the reform. After that is completed by about 2045, the surpluses go to reducing payroll taxes under an automatic payroll tax cut trigger specifically included in the bill. Under the chief actuary's score, the surpluses would be sufficient to reduce the total payroll tax eventually to about 4 percent, 2 percent each for employer and employee. Workers and employers would still contribute a total of 6.4 percent in addition for the accounts. But this is money that belongs to the workers in their own individual accounts, so it is not a tax that goes to the government. And remember that this is an alternative to raising the current 12.4 percent total payroll tax to 20 percent, as would be required to pay all benefits promised under the current law. *The Ryan–Sununu plan would be effectively the largest tax cut in world history.*

The reform would also greatly broaden the ownership of wealth and capital through the accounts. Under the chief actuary's score, workers would accumulate $7 trillion in today's dollars within the first fifteen years, by 2020. This huge, breakthrough gain in the prosperity of working people would have broad implications throughout our society.

Many more people would have an ownership stake in America's businesses. Support for free market policies would be shared more generally throughout our society. That would translate into more rapid economic growth and more prosperity for everyone, with no tax on the returns to the accounts, no tax on the benefits paid from the accounts, and no estate tax when account funds are left to children or other heirs.

The full potential economic gain from such reform has not been fully appreciated. All of the high-tech advances that beckon in the twenty-first century will require huge amounts of capital to achieve full practical application. The Ryan-Sununu reform will help provide the capital for a sweeping technology revolution that in turn will make returns on personal accounts potentially higher than we can predict using older models of economic growth.

Democrats argue against personal accounts by saying that workers should not be fooled into trading a guaranteed benefit (by which they mean the current Social Security benefits, which, in fact, are not guaranteed), for a speculative one (by which they mean personal account benefits). But the Ryan–Sununu plan does not involve any such trade-off. The legislation includes a federal guarantee that those with personal accounts would get at least as much as promised by Social Security today (which, again, the current system cannot pay, according to official government projections).

The cost of this guarantee was scored by the chief actuary of Social Security and is fully paid for under the reform plan. The guarantee works because capital market investment returns are so much higher than what Social Security promises; let alone what it can pay. Indeed, with workers choosing investments only from a list of fully diversified portfolios managed by top professional companies approved and regulated by the government, Peter Ferrara argues that even the chief actuary's estimated cost is surely excessive.

The Challenge of Historic Reform

For conservatives, such personal account reform could not be a bigger or more urgent issue. By shifting fundamentally all Social Security retirement benefits to the personal accounts over the long run, and financing part of the transition by reducing the rate of growth of federal spending, the Ryan–Sununu bill will ultimately reduce federal spending by roughly 6.5 percent of GDP. That, in fact, is a must if we are to avoid an explosion of federal spending relative to GDP that will result under current federal policies.

Personal accounts will in fact fulfill the promise that the Social Security system cannot deliver: a guaranteed retirement account. President Franklin Roosevelt and President Ronald Reagan would both be pleased.

For more information on Social Security personal accounts, visit **www.newt.org/winningthefuture**

Chapter 3

The Centrality of Our Creator in Defining America

There is no attack on American culture more deadly and more historically dishonest than the secular Left's unending war against God in America's public life. For me, the decision by the Ninth Circuit Court of Appeals to rule unconstitutional the phrase "one nation under God" was the final straw. A court that would destroy a Pledge of Allegiance adopted by the Congress, signed by the president (Eisenhower), and supported by 91 percent of the American people[1] is a court that is clearly out of step with an America that understands that our rights come from God, which is why no government—or court—can justly take them away from us.

While the Supreme Court overruled the Ninth Circuit on procedural grounds, it did not affirm that saying "one nation under God" was constitutional. Only three of the justices took that position. Five of the justices hid behind procedural excuses, ruling that the atheist plaintiff did not have legal standing to file the suit. The ninth justice, Antonin Scalia, had recused himself because he had made a public speech supporting the Pledge. Amazingly, today, the Supreme Court likely has a five to four majority for declaring "one nation under God" unconstitutional. Justice Sandra Day O'Connor defended the Pledge only by denying it any meaning: "even if taken literally, the phrase is merely descriptive; it purports only to identify the United States as a Nation subject to divine authority. That cannot be seen as a serious invocation of God or as an expression of individual submission to divine authority. . . . Any religious freight the words may have been meant to carry has long since been lost." The Pledge, she deemed, merely invoked "civic deism." Yet if *pledging allegiance* to one nation under God does not mean we believe the nation (and therefore ourselves as citizens) is under God, what could it possibly mean?

When a handful of judges decide they can overrule the culture of 91 percent of America, how can the Court maintain its moral authority? It can't. The Court itself begins each day with the proclamation, "God save the United States and this honorable Court." This phrase has been used for almost two hundred years. It was not adopted as a ceremonial phrase of no meaning; it was adopted because justices in the 1820s actually wanted to call on God to save the United States and the Court.

Similarly, the Pledge of Allegiance does not contain a "ceremonial" reference to God. The term under God was inserted deliberately by Congress to draw the distinction between atheistic tyranny (the Soviet Union) and a free society whose freedoms were based on the God-given rights of each person. As the report from the House of Representatives accompanying the law asserted: "From the time of our earliest history, our peoples and our institutions have reflected the traditional concept that our Nation was founded on a fundamental belief in God."

"Fundamental belief" is not "civic deism."

For most Americans, the blessings of God have been the basis of our liberty, prosperity, and survival as a unique country.

For most Americans, prayer is real and we subordinate ourselves to a God on whom we call for wisdom, salvation, and guidance.

For most Americans, an atheistic society that forbids public reference to God and removes religious symbols is a horrifyingly bad society.

Yet the voice of the overwhelming majority of Americans is repressed by an elite media that finds religious expression frightening and threatening, or old-fashioned and unsophisticated. The results of their opposition are everywhere.

Our schools have been steadily driving God out of American history (look at your children's textbooks or at the curriculum guide for your local school).

Our courts have been literally outlawing references to God, symbols of God, and stated public appeals to God (prayer).

For two generations we have passively accepted this assault on the values of the overwhelming majority of Americans. It is time to insist on judges who understand the history and meaning of America as a country endowed by God.

The secular Left has been inventing law and grotesquely distorting the Constitution to achieve a goal that none of the Founding Fathers would have thought reasonable. History is vividly clear about the importance of God in the founding of our nation. To prove that our Creator is so central to understanding America, I have developed a walking tour of Washington, D.C., to show how often the Founding Fathers and other great Americans, and the institutions they created, refer to God and call upon Him (appendix B). Indeed, to study American history is to encounter God again and again. A tour like this should be part of every school class's visit to Washington, D.C.

Religion is the fulcrum of American history. People came to America's shores to be free to practice their religious beliefs. It brought the Pilgrims with their desire to create a "city on a hill" that would be a beacon of religious belief and piety. The Pilgrims were but one group that poured into the new colonies. Quakers in Pennsylvania were another, Catholics in Maryland yet a third. A religious revival, the Great Awakening in the 1730s, inspired many Americans to fight the Revolutionary War to secure their God-given freedoms. Another great religious revival in the nineteenth century inspired the abolitionists' campaign against slavery.

It was no accident that the marching song of the Union Army during the Civil War included the line "as Christ died to make men holy let us die to make men free." That phrase was later changed to "let us live to make men free." But for the men in uniform who were literally placing their lives on the line to end slavery, they knew that the original line was the right one.

First Principles

For the colonists the argument with the British government was an argument about first principles. Where did power come from? What defined loyalty? Who defined rights between king and subject?

It was in this historic context that America proclaimed in the Declaration of Independence that all people "are endowed by their Creator with certain inalienable rights, that among these are life, liberty and the pursuit of happiness." This turned on its head the notion that power came from God through the monarch to the people.

Beginning with King John in 1215, the English had gradually been restricting and confining the power of their monarchs. But Americans went further, asserting that God granted rights directly to everyone. Moreover, these rights were "inalienable." The government could not deny man's God-given rights.

Those who came aboard the Mayflower in 1620 in search of religious freedom wrote a compact expressing that,

> We whose names are underwritten . . . by the grace of God . . . having undertaken, for the glory of God, and advancement of the Christian faith . . . a voyage to plant the first colony in the Northern parts of Virginia, do by these presents solemnly and mutually in the presence of God, and one of another, covenant and combine ourselves together into a civil body politic, for our better ordering and preservation and furtherance of the ends aforesaid; and by virtue hereof to enact, constitute, and frame such just and equal laws, ordinances, acts, constitutions, and offices, from time to time, as shall be thought most meet and convenient for the general good of the colony, unto which we promise all due submission and obedience.

At America's Founding, religion was central. The very first Continental Congress in 1774 had invited the Reverend Jacob Duché to begin each session with a prayer. When the war against Britain began, the Continental Congress provided for chaplains to serve with the military and be paid at the same rate as majors in the Army.

During the Constitutional Convention of 1787, Benjamin Franklin (often considered one of the least religious of the Founding Fathers) proposed that the Convention begin each day with a prayer. As the oldest delegate, at age eighty-one, Franklin insisted that "the longer I live, the more convincing proofs I see of this truth—that God governs in the Affairs of Men."

Because of their belief that power had come from God to the individual, they began the Constitution "we the people." Note that the Founding Fathers did not write "we the states." Nor did they write "we the government." Nor did they write "we the lawyers and judges."

These historic facts pose an enormous problem for secular liberals. How can they explain America without getting into the area of religion? If they dislike and in many cases fear religion, how then can they communicate the core nature of the people in America?

The answer is that modern secular liberalism cannot accurately teach or deal with religion as a central reality of American history, so it simply ignores the topic. If you don't teach about the Founding Fathers, you do not have to teach about our Creator. If you don't teach about Abraham Lincoln, you don't have to deal with fourteen references to God and two Bible verses in a 732–word second inaugural address. That speech is actually carved into the wall of the Lincoln Memorial in a permanent affront to every atheist who visits this public building. You have to wonder how soon there will be a lawsuit to scrape the references to God and the Bible off the monument so as not to offend those who hate or despise religion. This is no idle threat. Dr. Michael Newdow, the atheist who brought suit to outlaw the motto "one nation under God," told the *New York Times* he intended to "ferret out all insidious uses of religion in daily life."[2]

Unlike Dr. Newdow, the Founding Fathers, from the very birth of the United States, saw God as central to defining America. Professor Donald Lutz reviewed an estimated 15,000 items and 2,200 books, pamphlets, and newspaper articles with explicitly political content printed between 1760 and 1805. He counted 3,154 citations in the writings of the Founders; of these, nearly 1,100 references (34 percent) are to the Bible, and about 300 each are to Montesquieu and Blackstone, followed at considerable distance by Locke, Hume, and Plutarch.[3] Quite clearly, the original intent of the Founding Fathers in adopting *both* the Free Exercise and Establishment Clause was to promote religious freedom, not to suppress it.

Our first President, George Washington, at his first inauguration on April 30, 1789, "put his right hand on the Bible... [after taking the oath] adding 'So help me God.' He then bent forward and kissed the Bible before him."[4] In his inaugural address, Washington remarked that

> ... it would be peculiarly improper to omit in this first official act my fervent supplications to that Almighty Being who rules over the universe, who presides in the councils of nations, and whose providential aids can supply every human defect, that His benediction may consecrate to the liberties and happiness of the people of the United States a Government instituted by themselves for these essential purposes, and may enable every instrument employed in its administration to execute with success the functions allotted to his charge.... No people can be bound to acknowledge and adore the Invisible Hand which conducts the affairs of men more than those of the United States.... You will join with me, I trust, in thinking that there are none under the influence of which the proceedings of a new and free government can more auspiciously commence.

Then in the Thanksgiving Proclamation of October 3, 1789, Washington declared "it is the duty of all Nations to acknowledge the Providence of Almighty God, to obey His will, to be grateful for His benefits, and humbly to implore His protection and favor." Note that Washington was not just imploring that individuals have an obligation to God, but *nations* do as well. The United States government was not yet a year old.

Freedom of Religion; Not Freedom from Religion

The Bill of Rights was designed to protect freedom *of* religion not freedom *from* religion. Any serious look at the Founding Fathers and their behavior would reveal how much they believed in freedom *of* religion and how deeply they would have opposed government trying to create freedom *from* religion.

In writing the Northwest Ordinance in 1787, the Congress asserted "Religion, Morality, and knowledge being necessary to good government and the happiness of mankind, schools and the means of education shall be forever encouraged." Note that religion and morality precede knowledge as the purposes of school. Compare that with the secular, moral relativism of the modern education establishment.

Washington's successor, John Adams, warned that "it is Religion and Morality alone, which can establish the Principles upon which Freedom can securely stand."

The third and fourth presidents, Thomas Jefferson and James Madison, are usually considered the least religious of the early presidents, yet both attended church services in the Capitol. In fact, services were held in the House chamber until after the Civil War. At one point some 2,000 people were attending church in the Capitol, making our capitol building probably the largest church in the country. Jefferson also allowed executive branch buildings to be used for church services.

Jefferson was opposed to an official national religion but he was supportive of religion. The key was the term "Establishment of Religion." The secular Left looks to Jefferson's letter to the Danbury Baptists (January 1, 1802) in which he said there should be "a wall of separation between church and state." They then ignore the fact that two days later he went to the United States House of Representatives to attend church services. In fact one observer wrote that "Jefferson during his whole administration was a most regular attendant."[5]

Church did not just take place in the House chamber. During Jefferson's presidency church was also held in the Treasury building and in the Supreme Court. For those secular liberals who believe Jefferson did not believe in God, I always urge them to visit the Jefferson Memorial and read around the top: "I have sworn upon on the altar of God eternal hostility against every form of tyranny over the mind of man."

The issue of the Establishment Clause and its interpretation is at the heart of the question of God in American public life. The First Amendment is actually quite clear. It states, "Congress shall make no law respecting an establishment of religion, or prohibiting the free exercise thereof; or abridging the freedom of speech, or of the press; or the right of the people peaceably to assemble, and to petition the Government for a redress of grievances."

This language plainly refers to the question of establishing an official religion. Jefferson and Madison, by attending church in public buildings, clearly saw no conflict between opposing an official, state religion, and favoring religious observance in public places.

Jefferson took additional steps to indicate government support for religion in general. While president, Jefferson chaired the school board for the District of Columbia. He wrote the first plan of education adopted by the City of Washington, which used the Bible and Isaac Watt's Hymnal as the principal books to teach reading to students.

Jefferson recommended that Congress extend a treaty with the Kaskaskia Indians, which provided for annual support ($100) to a Catholic missionary priest to be paid out of the federal treasury.[6] Similar treaties were made with the Wyandotte and the Cherokee tribes. Jefferson extended three times the "Resolution granting lands to Moravian

Brethren," a 1787 act of Congress in which special lands were designated "for the sole use of Christian Indians and the Moravian Brethren missionaries for civilizing the Indians and promoting Christianity."

Jefferson not only signed bills that appropriated financial support for chaplains in Congress and in the armed services, but he also signed the Articles of War on April 10, 1806, in which he "Earnestly recommended to all officers and soldiers, diligently to attend divine services."

In establishing the University of Virginia, Jefferson encouraged the teaching of religion, and also set aside a place inside the Rotunda for chapel services. He also spoke highly of the use, in his hometown, of the local courthouse for religious services.

On one occasion, Jefferson declared that religion is "deemed in other countries incompatible with good government and yet proved by our experience to be its best support."[7]

This sense of the legitimacy of God in public places as seen by the Founding Fathers has a number of other historic facts to support it.

President Madison, the author of the Bill of Rights and the First Amendment, renewed the tradition of Thanksgiving Proclamations during the war of 1812. In 1814 Madison declared: "a day of... prayer to Almighty God for the safety and welfare of these States, His blessing to their arms."

In 1815 he proclaimed "a day... to be observed by the people of the United States with religious solemnity as a day of thanksgiving and of devout acknowledgment to Almighty God for His great goodness manifested in restoring to them the blessing of peace.... to the same Divine Author of Every Good and Perfect Gift we are indebted for all those privileges and advantages, religious as well as civil, which are so richly enjoyed in this favored land."

If the author of the First Amendment attended church in government buildings and issued proclamations thanking God for our deliverance, then where is the wall of separation the secular Left has been seeking to impose through a Supreme Court that has spent forty years denying the facts about the Constitution and American history?

James Madison authored the Bill of Rights in the First Congress. At the very time Congress was considering the First Amendment, which blocked "an establishment of religion," the same members of Congress were also hiring and paying for chaplains for the House and Senate.[8] If the members who authored the First Amendment did not believe it blocked them from paying public money for a chaplain and offering public prayers in a public building, then it is an absurdity for the Supreme Court to interpret the behavior of the Founding Fathers in writing the First Amendment as an anti-religious action. Everything we know about the Founders' individual and collective behavior indicates they were comfortable with God in public life and determined to recognize the religious basis of American liberty.

That most astute observer of early America, Alexis de Tocqueville, in *Democracy in America* (1835), observed "I do not know whether all Americans have a sincere faith in their religion, for who can read the human heart? But I am certain that they hold it to be indispensable to the maintenance of republican institutions. This opinion is not peculiar to a class of citizens or to a party, but it belongs to the whole nation and to every rank of society."

The secular Left and the Left-liberal elite media would argue that even if de Tocqueville were right, he is irrelevant because he is writing about an earlier America. They argue that America has changed profoundly and is now a very different country. Justice O'Connor herself wrote that the phrase "one nation under God" was adopted in 1954 when "our national religious diversity was neither as robust nor as well recognized as it is now."

Yet this is a profound misinterpretation of modern America. As Michael Novak has said to me, recognizing "one nation under God" is much more important in a country as religiously diverse as America because the phrase transcends any one faith or denomination and is as inclusive as possible. Harvard professor Samuel Huntington points out that "Americans tend to have a certain catholicity toward religion: All deserve respect. Given this tolerance of religious diversity, non-Christian faiths have little alternative but to recognize and accept America as a Christian society."[9]

The idea that somehow the phrase "under God" is only a fifty-year-old tradition is historically inaccurate. In an article in the *Weekly Standard* on October 27, 2003, James Piereson wrote that on July 2, 1776, as British troops were closing in on Staten Island and the Continental Congress was meeting in Philadelphia to declare independence, George Washington was gathering his troops in Long Island for battles in and around New York City. Washington wrote in the General Orders to his men that day, "The time is now near at hand which must probably determine whether Americans are to be freemen or slaves. . . . The fate of unborn millions will now depend, under God, on the courage and conduct of this army." The very same week we were declaring our independence, Washington was asserting that we, as a nation, served under God.

Abraham Lincoln, in his Gettysburg Address, remarked that

> It is for us the living, rather, to be dedicated here to the unfinished work which they who fought here have thus far so nobly advanced. It is rather for us to be here dedicated to the great task remaining before us—that from these honored dead we take increased devotion to the cause for which they gave the last full measure of devotion; that we here highly resolve that these dead shall not have died in vain; that this nation, under

> God, shall have a new birth of freedom; and that government of the people, by the people, for the people, shall not perish from the earth.

We are, and always have been, a nation "under God," regardless of our "robust national religious diversity." Statistically, Americans believe this as well. We are still overwhelmingly religious, believe in prayer, and are almost entirely within the Judeo-Christian tradition. Indeed, numerically this is a largely Christian country as it has been from its founding. The Pew Research Council in March 2002 found that 82 percent of Americans claim to be Christian.

Huntington goes on to assert:

> By the 1990s, Americans overwhelmingly supported a greater role for religion in American public life. In a 1991 survey, 78 percent of the respondents favored allowing children on school grounds to say prayers, to have voluntary Bible classes, and to hold meetings of voluntary Christian fellowship groups. Some 67 percent favored the display of nativity scenes or menorahs on government property; 73 percent approved prayers before athletic games; and 74 percent opposed removing all references to God from oaths of public office.[10]

He went on to note that only 11 percent (roughly equal to the proportion who say they are agnostic or atheist "thought it [religion] had too much" influence in American life.

De Tocqueville and the Founding Fathers would recognize the America Huntington describes. Huntington is chairman of the Harvard Academy for International and Area Studies and one of the most distinguished professors at a bastion of the secular Left. He is hardly a right-wing fanatic. Yet he asserts, "cultural America is under siege."[11]

Huntington believes it is possible for the vast majority to reassert American exceptionalism and insist on respect for and reinforcement of America's values and institutions. As Huntington suggests:

> America was founded in large part for religious reasons and religious movements have shaped its evolution for almost four centuries. By every indicator, Americans are far more religious than the people of other industrialized countries. Overwhelming majorities of white Americans, of black Americans, and of Hispanic Americans are Christians. In a world in which culture and particularly religion shape the allegiances, the alliances and the antagonisms of people on every continent, Americans could again find their national identity and their national purpose in their culture and religion.[12]

The two primary battlefields of this cultural struggle are the courts and the classrooms. Those are the arenas in which the secular Left has imposed change against the wishes of the overwhelming majority of Americans. Those are the arenas in which believing in the Founding Fathers and the classic interpretation of the Constitution can be disastrous to a career and lead to social ostracism.

If we insist on courts that follow the facts of American history in interpreting the Constitution, we will reestablish the right that every American has to acknowledge our Creator as the source of our rights, our well being, and our wisdom. And if we insist on patriotic education both for our children and for new immigrants, we will rebuild the cultural bond of historic memory that has made America the most exceptional nation in history.

For more information on the centrality of our Creator in defining America, visit **www.newt.org/winningthefuture**

Chapter 4

Bringing the Courts Back Under the Constitution

The defeat of judicial supremacy and a return to popular constitutionalism and a true balance of power between the legislative, executive, and judicial branches will be one of the most intense and difficult struggles of our lifetime. It is also absolutely unavoidable if we are going to retain our freedoms and our identity as Americans.

Over the last fifty years the Supreme Court has become a permanent constitutional convention in which the whims of five appointed lawyers have rewritten the meaning of the Constitution. Under this new all-powerful model of the Court, and by extension the trail-breaking Ninth Circuit Court, the Constitution and the law can be redefined with no boundaries.

The long, difficult process of amending the Constitution with its requirements for two-thirds majorities in Congress and for three-fourths of the states to concur was designed to make changing the Constitution very difficult. When I was Speaker we tried to get a balanced budget amendment and received the 290 votes necessary in the House but fell two votes short in the Senate. Even if the amendment had received the necessary votes in the Congress we would then have had to go to the states to secure thirty-eight states' ratification.

Yet all this effort is matched by a 5 to 4 vote on the Supreme Court. If five justices decide we cannot say "one nation under God," cannot pray at graduation, and cannot criticize politicians with campaign ads just before an election, then we lose those rights. If they decide that child pornography on the Internet is protected by free speech (unlike prayer and political speech) that becomes the law of the land. This power grab by the Court is a modern phenomenon and a dramatic break from all previous American history.

Where the Power Grab Leads: The Ninth Circuit Court of Appeals

Anyone who thinks the various decisions of the Supreme Court are not adequately worrisome need only look at the Ninth Circuit Court of Appeals to see how far the Left will go and how much domination by secular Left judges will change America.

It is almost unimaginable that one court could be so out of step with American values and the views of the vast majority of the American people. And it is almost inconceivable that this destructive pattern could have been going on for a generation without an effective response from the president or the Congress.

Consider the following Ninth Circuit decisions:

- *Elk Grove Unified School District v. Newdow* (2002): The Ninth Circuit ruled that "one nation under God" in the Pledge of

Allegiance was unconstitutional. It was later overruled on procedural grounds by the Supreme Court.

- *Silveira v. Lockyer* (2002): The Ninth Circuit held there is no individual right to keep and bear arms.
- *Andrade v. Attorney General of California* (2001): The Ninth Circuit said the California three-strikes law was unconstitutional; the Supreme Court reversed it.
- *Summerlin v. Stewart* (2003): The Ninth Circuit said *Ring v. Arizona*'s rule that a death sentence must be enacted by jury, and not judge, applied retroactively, and subsequently voided the death sentences of over 100 inmates. The other circuit courts found that the rule did not apply retroactively. The Supreme Court reversed it.
- *Rucker v. Davis* (2001): Under the law in question, tenants in public housing could be evicted if one member of the family were involved in drug activity at or near the complex. The full Ninth Circuit ruled that the law did not apply to people who did not have prior knowledge of the criminal behavior. The Supreme Court reversed it. Congress specifically addressed this situation.
- *Compassion in Dying v. Washington* (1995): The full Ninth Circuit declared a constitutional right to assisted suicide. The Supreme Court reversed it.
- *U.S. v. Oakland Cannabis Buyers Cooperative* (1999): The full Ninth Circuit found a "medical necessity" exemption to the federal Controlled Substances Act. The Supreme Court reversed it.
- *Yniguez v. Arizonans for Official English* (1995): The Ninth Circuit held an Arizona amendment requiring state business to be conducted in English violated the First Amendment.

When a Court is reversed this often, it clearly fails to meet the "good behavior" test of the Constitution—a narrow version of the Judiciary Act of 1802 by which the Jeffersonians simply disestablished a majority of the existing federal circuit judges. The good behavior test should be enforced. It would certainly focus the Ninth Circuit's attention on survival rather than radicalism. Yet far from wanting the courts to pull back or become more cautious, many on the Left want the courts to take over bigger and bigger portions of the duties that were historically part of the legislative and executive branches.

The Left Wants the Courts to Be Even More Aggressive

Former Secretary of Labor Robert Reich recently made clear how much he thinks the courts should be relied upon by liberals:

> In the old days, state legislatures or Congress would enact laws, which would be administered by regulatory agencies. But now the era of big government is over. "Regulation" is a bad word. So how are these regulatory issues being handled? Through lawsuits. . . . In his State of the Union Address, President Clinton announced he wanted the Justice Department to sue tobacco companies as well, in order to collect billions of dollars that Medicare spends caring for people with smoking-related illnesses. . . . Many legal experts doubt the federal government has the authority to launch such a lawsuit. But that's irrelevant. The lawsuit would be a bargaining chip for settling the case. . . . The era of big government may be over, but the era of regulation through litigation has just begun.[1]

The *New York Times* is even more enthusiastic than Robert Reich about the opportunity for the courts to overrule the state legislators, the governors, and the Congress and do their job for them. In a July 11, 2004, editorial, they wrote:

> Too often, felon voting is seen as a partisan issue. In state legislatures, it is usually Democrats who try to restore voting rights, and Republicans who resist. . . . The treatment of former felons in the electoral system cries out for reform. . . . Restoring the vote to felons is difficult, because it must be done state by state, and because ex-convicts do not have much of a political lobby. . . . The best hope of reform may lie in the courts. The Atlanta-based United States Court of Appeals for the Eleventh Circuit and the San Francisco–based Court of Appeals for the Ninth Circuit have ruled recently that disenfranchising felons may violate equal protection or the Voting Rights Act.

None of the Founding Fathers expected the courts to ever have the arrogance to reach into the legislative and executive branches and begin writing law and redefining America. In fact, the Founding Fathers believed the judicial branch was the weakest branch and the least likely to pose a threat to the Constitution and to our liberties.

Safeguarding Liberty: The Historic Balance Among the Three Branches

Historically there was a balance of power between the three branches of the federal government, as the Constitution provided and the *Federalist Papers* explicitly described.

Alexander Hamilton expected the legislative branch would define the reach of the judicial branch. He argued in Federalist 80 that when the judiciary had to be modified, "the national legislature will have ample authority to make such exceptions, and to prescribe such regulations as will be calculated to obviate or remove these inconveniences."

Hamilton was also confident the judiciary branch would never encroach upon the legislative branch. He noted in Federalist 81, "There can never be any danger that the judges, by a series of deliberate usurpations on the authority of the legislature, would hazard the united resentment of the body entrusted with it, while this body was possessed of the means of punishing their presumption by degrading them from their stations."

Where Hamilton had relied on the legislature's power to respond, James Madison argued for the theory of a division of power into three branches based on Montesquieu: "Were the power of judging joined with the legislative, the life and liberty of the subject would be exposed to arbitrary control, for the judge would then be the legislator. Were it joined to the executive power, the judge might behave with all the violence of an oppressor."

Madison goes on to argue in Federalist 48,

> . . . that the powers properly belonging to one of the departments ought not to be directly and completely administered by either of the other departments. It is equally evident, that none of them ought to possess, directly or indirectly, an overruling influence over the others, in the administration of their respective powers. It will not be denied, that power is of an encroaching nature, and that it ought to be effectually restrained from passing the limits assigned to it. After discrimi-

> nating, therefore, in theory, the several classes of power, as they may in their nature be legislative, executive, or judiciary, the next and most difficult task is to provide some practical security for each, against the invasion of the others.

Madison feared that the legislative branch would be the primary source of encroaching on the power of the other branches. He was wrong.

The Power Grab of the Lawyer Class: The Oligarchy Jefferson Feared

The lawyer class began a grand-scale power grab with the Warren Court in the 1950s. Larry Kramer, dean at the Stanford Law School, captures the sudden dramatic shift in the Warren Court's interpretation of judicial supremacy:

> In 1958 . . . all nine Justices signed an extraordinary opinion in *Cooper v. Aaron* insisting that *Marbury* [*Marbury v. Madison*] had "declared the basic principle that the federal judiciary is supreme in the exposition of the law of the Constitution" and that this idea "has ever since been respected by this Court and the Country as a permanent and indispensable feature of our constitutional system." This was, of course, just bluster and puff. As we have seen, *Marbury* said no such thing, and judicial supremacy was not cheerfully embraced in the years after *Marbury* was decided. The Justices in *Cooper* were not reporting a fact so much as trying to manufacture one . . . the declaration of judicial interpretive

> supremacy evoked considerable skepticism at the time. But here is the striking thing: after *Cooper v. Aaron*, the idea of judicial supremacy seemed gradually, at long last, to find wide public acceptance.[2]

Having declared the Supreme Court superior to the legislative and executive branches, the members of the Court now live in a world in which they have no peers. Lord Acton had warned in the mid-nineteenth century that "power tends to corrupt and absolute power corrupts absolutely." Note that he drops the "tends" in describing the impact of absolute power.

The Warren Court was determined to break with previous Supreme Courts and the traditions of American history to define a much more radical America. Its prime target was religion.

Justice Hugo Black had laid the groundwork in *Everson v. Board of Education* (1947). Justice Black used a narrow case: Could New Jersey fund transportation for children to get to Catholic schools as well as public schools? But in doing so, he helped to create the sweeping principle that would turn the Establishment Clause of the First Amendment into a bulldozer for creating a secular America. He wrote:

> The "establishment of religion" clause of the First Amendment means at least this: Neither a state nor the Federal Government can set up a church. Neither can pass laws which aid one religion, aid all religions, or prefer one religion over another. Neither can force nor influence a person to go to or to remain away from church against his will or force him to profess a belief or disbelief in any religion. No person can be punished for entertaining or professing religious beliefs or disbeliefs, for church attendance or non-attendance. No tax in any amount, large

> or small, can be levied to support any religious activities or institutions, whatever they may be called, or whatever form they may adopt to teach or practice religion. Neither a state nor the Federal Government can, openly or secretly, participate in the affairs of any religious organizations or groups and vice versa. In the words of Jefferson, the clause against establishment of religion by law was intended to erect "a wall of separation between Church and State."

This is a fundamental misreading of Jefferson—who did not believe there should be a wall between God and state but only between an established religion and the government.

As Michael Novak, author of the wonderful book *On Two Wings*, has observed:

> From 1776 to 1948, the dominant metaphor for church-state relations was that public officials must act as "nursing fathers" to the religious and moral habits of the people (the phrase in quotes comes from Isaiah). Jefferson's phrase "wall of separation" from a letter of 1802 lay totally unnoticed until it was cited by the Supreme Court in 1879 in *Reynolds v. United States* in a mistaken transcription of Jefferson's original letter; the focus in 1879 was not on "separation" but on the term "*legislative* powers" (which the transcriber had written instead of Jefferson's original clearly formed handwriting "*legitimate* power"). The metaphor otherwise lay unused and virtually unknown until Justice Black drew it from obscurity in 1947 (still using the erroneous translation.)[3]

James Hutson also provides interesting details on this often overlooked piece of history:

> [That Jefferson] supported throughout his life the principle of government hospitality to religious activities (provided always that it be voluntary and offered on an equal-opportunity basis) indicates that he used the wall of separation metaphor in a restrictive sense.... government, although it could not take coercive initiatives in the religious sphere, might serve as a passive, impartial venue for voluntary religious activities.[4]

Justice Black had asserted a ruthlessly secular, anti-religious definition of the Establishment Clause and it became the benchmark for future decisions.

The next big break with tradition came in 1962 when the Supreme Court in *Engel v. Vitale* struck down a New York State law that required school officials to open the day with prayer. Justice Potter Stewart's dissent cited examples of the "deeply entrenched and highly cherished spiritual traditions of our nation." As Justice Stewart noted, we "are a religious people whose institutions presuppose a Supreme Being."

Presciently, Justice Douglas concurred in the majority but noted its ominous implications:

> What New York does on the opening of its public schools is what we do when we open court. Our Crier has from the beginning announced the convening of the Court. God Save the United States and this Honorable Court. That utterance is a supplication, a prayer in which we, the judges, are free to join, but which we need not recite any more than the students need to recite the New York prayer. What New York does on the opening of its public schools is what each House of Congress does at the opening of each day's business.

Most people ignored Douglas's observation at the time but we now know they should have taken it very seriously. The line was being crossed from a pro-religious nation to an anti-religious nation and with each judgment the momentum of secularism accelerated.

In the 1963 decision *Abington v. Schempp*, the Supreme Court ruled that Bible reading in schools was unconstitutional. This case is widely regarded as the decisive break in which the Court began to use the Establishment Clause of the First Amendment to drive religion out of public life. Even those who sought to retain some reference to America's religious origin and the religious basis of the rights of Americans began doing so in the context of an acceptance of a sanitized, secular, non-religious public life.

The theme that God can remain in public life as long as He is not taken seriously was established in this case. Justice Arthur Goldberg noted that no practice is prohibited if it does not "have meaningful and practical impact." He went on to assert that acts could remain constitutional as long as they remained a "mere shadow" of religious reference and were not a "real threat." Note that God had gone from the source of salvation (personal and national), inspiration, and wisdom to being a "threat" that could be tolerated only if the threat was tiny and timid.

In the same case Justice William Brennan noted that patriotic exercises such as the Pledge of Allegiance were fine because "they had lost any religious significance through repetitive usage." In other words, God could survive in public only as long as no one thought the reference actually meant God. Here is Justice Brennan's reasoning:

> This general principle might also serve to insulate the various patriotic exercises and activities used in the public schools and elsewhere which,

> whatever may have been their origins, no longer have a religious purpose or meaning. The reference to divinity in the revised pledge of allegiance, for example, may merely recognize the historical fact that our Nation was believed to have been founded "under God." Thus reciting the pledge may be no more of a religious exercise than the reading aloud of Lincoln's Gettysburg Address, which contains an allusion to the same historical fact.[5]

Justice Brennan made clear the break with the Founding Fathers and with American history: "A too literal quest for the advice of the Founding Fathers upon the issues of these cases seems to me futile and misdirected."

Justice Potter Stewart filed the only dissent and asserted,

> If religious exercises are held to be an impermissible activity in schools, religion is placed in an artificial and state-created disadvantage. . . . And a refusal to permit religious exercises thus is seen, not as the realization of state neutrality, but rather as the establishment of a religion of secularism, or at least, as governmental support of the beliefs of those who think that religious exercises should be conducted only in private.

Precedent: A One-Way Street to the Left

When the Left-liberal establishment claims that it is only following precedent, it is important to note that precedent only exists if it is in the Left's interest. Conservative precedents simply become mistakes to be rectified or inaccurate opinions to be corrected.

On the issue of religion in American public life, consider the precedents the modern Supreme Court has had to ignore in order to drive God out of public life.

Justice Joseph Story in a speech at Harvard in 1829 claimed, "there never has been a period of history in which the Common Law did not recognize Christianity as lying at its foundation." Justice Story wrote this into Court language in *Vidal v. Girard's Executors* (1844): "It is also said, and truly that the Christian religion is a part of the common law."

In 1890 the Supreme Court ruled against polygamy by asserting, "it is contrary to the spirit of Christianity and the civilization which Christianity has produced in the Western world."

In 1892 the Supreme Court noted, "Christianity, general Christianity, is and always has been, a part of the common law of Pennsylvania . . . not Christianity with an established church and tithes and spiritual courts, but Christianity with liberty of conscience to all men. . . . this is a Christian nation."

In 1931 the Supreme Court cited its 1892 language "We are a Christian people," and asserted that the government must make decisions in the belief that these decisions "are not inconsistent with the will of God."

In 1952, in sustaining a New York State law that allowed students to be released during the school day to go for religious instruction with their parents' consent, Justice Douglas asserted, "We are a religious people and our institutions presuppose a Supreme Being. . . . When the state encourages religious instruction or cooperates with religious authorities by adjusting the schedule of public events to sectarian needs, it follows the best of our traditions. We cannot read into the Bill of Rights a philosophy of hostility to religion."

These precedents make it clear that a new majority on the Court could reach back to earlier precedents and reestablish with ease the right to voluntary school prayer, the right to post the Ten Commandments, the right to have a prayer before graduations and athletic events, and other activities that would reestablish our right to recognize and appeal to God in public places.

Where Does the Supreme Court Look for Precedents Today?

Since it is clear that the modern Supreme Court has been ignoring both American history and the precedents set by earlier courts, where does it look for guidance?

Justice Antonin Scalia has asked this question of the Court: "What secret knowledge, one must wonder, is breathed into lawyers when they become Justices of this Court? Day by day, case by case, [the Court] is busy designing a Constitution for a country I do not recognize."

Justice Scalia went on, in dissenting from *United States v. Virginia*, to charge "this most illiberal Court, which has embarked on a course of inscribing one after another of the current preferences of the society (and in some cases only the counter-majoritarian preferences of the society's law-trained elite) into our Basic Law."

As Judge Robert H. Bork noted,

> Scalia understates how radical an antidemocratic course the Court has taken. The Justices are not inscribing current preferences of our society into the Constitution, for those preferences can be easily placed in statute by legislatures. When the Court declares a statute unconstitu-

> tional it overrides current popular desires. The counter-majoritarian preferences are not simply those of a law-trained elite, but those of a wider cultural elite that includes journalists, academics, entertainers, and the like. If only a law-trained elite were involved, the Court could not do what it is doing.[6]

Judge Bork went on to charge: "A judge who departs from the Constitution . . . is applying no law other than his will. Our country is being radically altered, step by step, by Justices who are not following any law."

If the current Supreme Court justices are no longer bound by the words of the Constitution and no longer studying either traditional precedents, American history, or the views of the Founding Fathers, then where do they get the inspiration to continue to radically rewrite America's laws?

The Growing Influence of Foreign Opinion

There is a new and growing pattern among the Left-liberal establishment to view foreign opinion and international organizations as more reliable and more legitimate than American institutions.

In July 2004, about a dozen House members wrote a letter to United Nations Secretary General Kofi Annan asking him to certify the 2004 presidential election. When an amendment was offered to block any federal official involving the U.N. in the American elections, the Democrats voted 160 to 33 in favor of allowing the U.N. to be called into an American election. The Republicans voted 210 to 0 against allowing the United Nations to interfere.

The fact that a five-to-one margin of Democrats could vote in favor of United Nations involvement in an American presidential election is an astonishing indicator of the degree to which international institutions have acquired greater legitimacy among the Left-liberal establishment.

This same trend toward the reliance of foreign opinion and foreign institutions is also developing in the Supreme Court.

Justice O'Connor, in 1997, argued, "Other legal systems continue to innovate, to experiment, and to find new solutions to the new legal problems that arise each day, from which we can learn and benefit." Later, in 2002, she further asserted: "There is much to learn from... distinguished jurists [in other places] who have given thought to the same difficult issues we face here."

Justice Ruth Bader Ginsberg, in 2003, stated:

> [O]ur "island" or "lone ranger" mentality is beginning to change. Our Justices... are becoming more open to comparative and international law perspectives. Last term may prove a milestone in that regard. *New York Times* reporter Linda Greenhouse observed on July 1 in her annual roundup of the Court's decisions: The Court has displayed a [steadily growing] attentiveness to legal developments in the rest of the world and to the Court's role in keeping the United States in step with them.

In other words, Justice Ginsberg is promising that as elites in other countries impose elite values on their people, the Supreme Court has the power and the duty to translate their new Left-liberal values on the American people. No more worrying about the legislative and executive branches. No more messy process of debating with the

American people. No more old-fashioned defense of American traditions and American constitutional precedent.

Justice Ginsberg quotes approvingly Justice Kennedy's opinion making same-sex relationships a constitutional right in part out of "respect for the Opinions of [Human]kind." The Court emphasized: "The right the petitioners seek in this case has been accepted as an integral part of human freedom in many other countries.... In support, the Court cited the leading 1981 European Court of Human Rights decision...and the follow-on European Human Rights Court decisions."

Justice Scalia dissented strongly, writing that Constitutional entitlements cannot come from foreign governments: "Much less do they spring into existence, as the Court seems to believe, because foreign nations decriminalize conduct." Scalia went on to assert that "this Court...should not impose foreign moods, fads, or fashions on Americans."

In a 2002 case (*Atkins v. Virginia*), Chief Justice Rehnquist also dissented: "I fail to see, however, how the views of other countries regarding the punishment of their citizens provide any support for the Court's ultimate determination...we have...explicitly rejected the idea that the sentencing practices of other countries could serve to establish the first Eighth Amendment prerequisite, that [a] practice is accepted among our people."

Despite these dissents, the majority on the Court is continuing to look outside America for guidance in interpreting American law.

In her own actions, Justice Ginsberg noted that in the Michigan affirmative action cases, "I looked to two United Nations Conventions: the 1965 International Convention on the Elimination of all Forms of Racial Discrimination, which the United States has ratified;

and the 1979 Convention on the Elimination of all Forms of Discrimination Against Women, which, sadly, the United States has not yet ratified. . . . The Court's decision in the Law School case, I observed, accords with the international understanding of the office of affirmative action." Note that Justice Ginsberg is proudly stating her use of a United Nations Convention which the United States Senate has not yet ratified.

Thus a mechanism has been locked into place by which five appointed lawyers can redefine the meaning of the U.S. Constitution and the policies implemented under that Constitution either by inventing rationales out of thin air or by citing whatever foreign precedent they think helpful. This is not a judiciary in the classic sense, but a proto-dictatorship of the elite pretending to still function as a Supreme Court.

Is the Judiciary Supreme in Interpreting the Constitution?

At the heart of the current grasp for power is the issue of whether the judiciary is truly the supreme interpreter of the Constitution.

Larry Kramer has rightly pointed out that the Founding Fathers would have certainly challenged the current Supreme Court in a variety of ways. President Thomas Jefferson was the first American leader to confront a hostile judiciary. The Federalists had used the federal judiciary to enforce the Alien and Sedition Acts of 1798 to imprison Jeffersonian activists. After the Federalists lost the election of 1800, they had from November until March 1801 (back then inauguration did not occur until March) to try to slow down the emerging Jeffersonian majority. The Federalists more than doubled the number of federal circuit judges (from seventeen to thirty-five), picked the judges, and had their departing Senate majority approve the new Federalist judges. Thus the Federalists prepared to give up power confident they had boxed in the new majority.

The Jeffersonians reacted to this post-election court packing with fury. They called the new appropriators Midnight Judges. In the Judiciary Act of 1802 they eliminated all eighteen new federal circuit court judgeships. They passed the act by very large majorities (better than two to one in the House). In the election of 1802 the Jeffersonians increased their majority over the Federalists in a campaign that further strengthened the legislative and executive branches against the judicial branch.

The Supreme Court ruled that this action was within Congress's constitutional powers under Article III in *Stuart v. Laird*.

Jefferson was quite clear about the absurdity of claims to judicial supremacy: "You seem . . . to consider the judges as the ultimate arbiters of all constitutional questions; a very dangerous doctrine indeed, and one which would place us under the despotism of an oligarchy."[7] Jefferson warned that "the germ of dissolution of our federal government is in the constitution of the federal judiciary, an irresponsible body, (for impeachment is scarcely a scare-crow) working like gravity by night and day, gaining a little today and a little tomorrow, and advancing its noiseless step like a thief, over the field of jurisdiction, until all shall be usurped from the States, and the government of all be consolidated into one."[8]

Jefferson further wrote that "the great object of my fear is the federal judiciary. That body, like gravity, ever acting, with noiseless foot, and unalarming advance, gaining ground step by step, and holding what it gains, is engulfing insidiously the special governments into the jaws of that which feeds them." The Jeffersonians had asserted unequivocally that the legislative and executive branches were coequals of the judiciary branch and that when two of the three branches were united, they could in effect trump the third branch.

President Andrew Jackson similarly interposed the executive branch against the Supreme Court in responding to one decision in 1831 by commenting, "John Marshall has made his decision; let him enforce it now if he can."

Abraham Lincoln reentered politics largely in response to the Supreme Court's *Dred Scott* decision enforcing slavery throughout the United States. Lincoln saw the Supreme Court decision as an assault on the freedom of all Americans. He also explicitly said he believed the Court was acting as part of a conspiracy involving President James Buchanan and Senator Stephen Douglas to achieve by Court decision what they could not achieve in the Congress.

Lincoln's entire presidential campaign was driven by his opposition to the extension of slavery embodied in the Supreme Court's decision. In many ways it could be argued that the Supreme Court created the legal setting in which the people of the United States had to settle what their Constitution meant and that settling this argument required a civil war. During the Civil War, Lincoln simply ignored the Supreme Court for war-imposed reasons and asserted that his responsibilities as commander in chief outweighed his obligation to obey the Court.

When Franklin Delano Roosevelt found the Supreme Court consistently throwing out New Deal legislation, he attempted to pack the Court with additional Supreme Court justices. While Roosevelt ultimately lost the battle in Congress, the assault had so intimidated the conservative justices that they shifted their opinions dramatically to accommodate the views of the vast majority of the American people as expressed in their votes for president and Congress. Roosevelt lost the battle but won the war.

Thus there is significant precedent in American history for believing that the legislative and executive branches can force the judicial branch into changing its views when they are out of touch with the values of the vast majority of Americans. What then should we do in our generation to return the Supreme Court and the other federal courts to making decisions that reinforce American values and American traditions?

Reestablishing a Traditional Judiciary

There is a sense of defeatism among the American people when it comes to the federal courts. People get angry but then give up because the Left-liberal media insist on judicial supremacy and assert that the only way to correct the Courts is to pass a constitutional amendment. Since drawing together 290 House members, sixty-seven senators, and thirty-seven states is a difficult and time-consuming task, the American people lose their interest, shrug their shoulders, and give up on the fight. In fact, there are some major steps we can take through the legislative and executive branches.

Americans can ask that Congress pass a law insisting on the centrality of "our Creator" in defining American rights, the legitimacy of appeals to God "in public places," and the absolute rejection of judicial supremacy as a violation of the Constitution's balance of powers. If the Supreme Court ruled that such a law was unconstitutional, the legislative and executive branches should retaliate. The Founding Fathers always believed that in a struggle between the popularly elected branches and the appointed branch, the judges would inevitably lose. Congress and the president should pass the law a second time but include a provision that affirms the legislative and executive branches' constitutional role to define the Court's jurisdiction. If this does not convince the judges, the legislative and executive branches have additional options. The American people can insist on electing senators who promise to confirm judges who enforce the Constitution as written.

Americans can also insist that judges who consistently ignore the Constitution fall short of the Constitution's "good behavior" clause. Thus the Ninth Circuit judges who found the motto "one nation under God" unconstitutional could be considered unfit to serve and be impeached.

If impeachment proves too radical or too difficult, the legislative and executive branches could combine to follow the Jeffersonian example and simply eliminate judgeships that consistently violate the Constitution. Thus much of the Ninth Circuit could find itself without a court to serve on.

The people can appeal to their state legislatures to call on Congress and the president to act every time the courts infringe on their liberties, traditions, and history. If there was a nationwide watchdog committee monitoring the courts and engaging the state legislatures whenever the courts behave radically, judges might think twice about radicalizing our laws.

Some people will read this and conclude these strategies are too bold. But if we don't act boldly, the secular leftists will continue to curtail our liberties and force their beliefs on us. We must either change the judiciary, or live in a different America. I prefer to preserve America and change the judiciary.

Creating a 21st Century System of Civil Justice

Edwards Deming once warned that litigation was one of the greatest threats to the American economy. Prior to 1963, civil justice suits were a reasonable part of making America work. Americans expected contracts to be enforced and rights to be protected. The law was the system by which we maintained our ability to function both in public and private activity. Only in the last forty years has the prospect of litigation emerged as a self-enriching industry for a narrow group of lawyers—the personal injury attorneys. Today, entire law firms exist solely to file such lawsuits. The scale of lawyer enrichment has grown to a point that some of the wealthiest men in America are personal injury lawyers who participated in the tobacco settlement. Money that should have gone to those injured by smoking instead went to lawyers who now fly their own private airplanes and buy baseball teams.

There are several major consequences of this explosion of litigation.

Laws are being changed from an instrument of justice into an instrument of revenge and redistribution. Americans are learning to treat litigation as a lottery, to sue rather than settle, and to turn American civil life into one of conflict and suspicion.

Venue shopping, a corrupt process by which personal injury lawyers seek out judges and juries who favor their case, is one way personal injury lawyers seek self-enrichment reliance rather than justice. The personal injury awards are often so large that the defendant has to bargain simply to avoid bankruptcy during the appeals process.

Class action lawsuits have become a terrifying nightmare for productive companies while doing remarkably little for the individuals supposedly harmed. People can even join a lawsuit by simply filling out a coupon at no cost, no risk, and with no need to prove an injury (they simply become part of the "class" filing suit).

Investment decisions about creating new drugs, jobs, and trying new services are being made riskier by defense lawyers who warn about the litigation that has unpredictable and possibly bankrupting costs. This endangers the entrepreneurial character of our economy.

Potential investors, looking at the litigation risks in America compared to the rest of the world, are beginning to shift investments to less risky countries.

Bright young Americans are learning that it is better to sue than to be sued, and as a result many young potential doctors, entrepreneurs, and scientists are going to law school instead of pursuing a healing or creating profession.

Reforming this system is made more difficult because Hollywood, the academic Left, and much of the elite media see the personal injury lawyers as allies in their opposition to the supposedly evil and selfish business and professional community.

As personal injury lawyers have grown richer, they have become more powerful and better able to protect their own interest in our litigious system. The personal injury bar has great influence in the United States Senate (having surpassed the labor unions as a major source of money for the Democrats), and therefore passing serious federal litigation reform has become an enormous undertaking.

One of the major mistakes made by critics of the litigation explosion has been to create an ad hominem anti-lawyer and anti-lawsuit mentality. Americans believe deeply in the right to go to court. Americans instinctively believe that their property rights and their protection against personal injury are embedded in the law.

The lawyer as officer of the court is central to the American system of civil and criminal justice. An anti-lawyer policy is, in the end, an anti–rule of law policy. And an anti-lawsuit policy is ultimately anti-the weak and injured. This deep cultural belief in the rule of law and the right to be protected by lawsuit is a reservoir the personal injury lawyers have reverted to again and again when litigation reform has been on the ballot or during debate in the state and federal legislatures.

We need to offer a positive vision of a 21st century system of civil justice that will both protect the individual and allow us to compete in the world market. The following are a series of principles that should frame such a system.

Everyone should know that rapid, inexpensive arbitration is preferable to litigation. Cases involving technical knowledge should go first to panels of experts (health courts in the case of medical malpractice), but plaintiffs should be able to appeal to a court if they feel cheated. They should, however, have to carry the result of the expert panel with them into the litigation.

Losers should be at risk for costs, and if the judge finds that the loser filed a case without substance, triple damages should be payable by the loser, and the personal injury lawyer should be required to pay court costs for having willfully brought a case without merit.

The injured party should be guaranteed 85 percent of the settlement while the personal injury lawyers should be limited to no more than 15 percent.

Class action lawsuits should be limited to people with legitimate complaints of serious personal harm. Just as you could not get into court for a tiny injury, you should not be able to enter a class action lawsuit for only a supposed problem or a tiny complaint. All activities of the class action lawsuit should be open to public scrutiny and the public should know what share of the total costs went to the injured parties and what share went to the lawyers as expenses and awards (remember that a 15 percent cap on the settlement will lead to a dramatic increase in attorney "expenses" as they seek ways to keep more of the money). The expenses should be auditable by a court administrator to ensure the attorneys are not misusing the injured parties' money.

It should be illegal for a law firm to form a class action lawsuit for its own enrichment. The injured parties should originate the lawsuits and hire the law firm. The judge should have the option of opening the class action lawsuit to competitive bidding to find the least expensive law firm for the injured parties.

Unless there is a clear and unmistakable venue of injury, the plaintiff and the defendant should have to negotiate a neutral venue for a multi-state case. The practice of venue shopping by personal injury lawyers looking for a friendly judge and jury has to be replaced by some system of seeking neutral sites with neutral judges and juries. Some kind of "striking" system comparable to jury selection might be the next stage for venue selection except in cases where the site of the injury is local and clear.

We should return to a world in which lawyers do not advertise. There are profound reasons why society has historically held that lawyers should not publicly seek cases. The damage done by constant thirty-second reminders of the right to sue and the right to feel injured and trespassed upon is incalculable. It actively harms American society, the American economy, and the stature and prestige of the legal profession. The profession-enhancing rationale behind anti–ambulance chasing laws was right. The reduction of the law into a commercial venture is wrong. It is time to reverse that decision and make the law once again above the profit motive.

We need more scientists, doctors, and entrepreneurs, and fewer lawyers, and we should do everything we can to make America a less litigious society—which will lead to fewer lawyers and more job creators and opportunity builders.

With these steps we will have begun to create a twenty-first century system of civil justice that provides faster solutions, awards the injured a vastly larger sum, reduces the negative effects on our economy and competitiveness, and still guarantees Americans the right to justice.

For more information on bringing the courts back under our Constitution, visit **www.newt.org/winningthefuture**

CHAPTER 5

PATRIOTIC IMMIGRATION

I DO NOT WORRY about people who want to come to the United States to work hard, pay taxes, obey the law, and become Americans. In fact, I am delighted to have new Americans join our country because historically they have been the source of enormous talent, energy, and courage. From Alexander Hamilton to Andrew Carnegie to Albert Einstein to Henry Kissinger to Arnold Schwarzenegger, people who wanted to improve their lives, and in the process improve the country, have enriched America.

Nor am I concerned that a substantial number of new Americans are Hispanic. America has a long history of absorbing and blending people of many languages and backgrounds. There have always been non-English newspapers in America and now we have non-English radio and television. I am also not worried that some immigrants come here only to earn money and then go home (Italian immigrants, in particular, did that in the past).

What worries me is the breakdown of will on the part of America to control our borders and to ensure that new immigrants learn to be American.

Controlling the Border

No serious nation in the age of terror can afford to have wide-open borders with millions of illegal aliens crossing at will.

But along with making it much harder to sneak in, we need to make it easier for guest workers to enter the country legally and to work here as long as they obey the law. Millions of illegal immigrants are here because Americans are hiring them. They have jobs in your neighborhood and you know it. They may be serving you lunch at a restaurant, washing your car, and mowing your lawn. They are probably working on the construction projects you drive past each day. Keeping these hard-working people illegal makes them vulnerable to criminals and keeps them from playing responsible roles in our communities.

We need a guest worker program to ensure that guest workers pay taxes, get driver's licenses, buy auto insurance, abide by the law, and that filters out criminals and potential terrorists. The program should not be an automatic qualification for citizenship, though eventual citizenship should be held out as an opportunity.

Patriotic Citizenship

Before we declare immigrants citizens, we need to go back and remember how to turn immigrants into citizens. For much of American history, states ran Americanization programs designed to help immigrants assimilate into American culture. In the last two generations the liberal establishment has undermined and ridiculed American values, American history, and even the idea of American citizenship. Today, leftists in the Democrat Party want voting opened to non-citizens, including illegal aliens. The Left regards national identity as irrelevant and patriotic commitment to America as irrelevant. The Left could not be further removed from the thinking of our Founding Fathers.

Dr. John Fonte, America's leading expert on civic education, explains the Founding Fathers' thoughts on how to make good citizens:

> First, as noted, they had to think about the young. After all, children were not born republican citizens, but would have to be taught how to become citizens. Second, they had to think about immigrants, how best should these newcomers become American citizens? Their answer was clear and unequivocal: immigrants should be assimilated into American ideas and American common culture. Hence, the Founders regularly used words associated with ideas ("principles," "beliefs") and words associated with the common civic culture ("habits," "customs," "manners," "language," "laws," "our society").[1]

Fonte noted that George Washington worried about large numbers of immigrants not assimilating. In a letter to John Adams he wrote that "... the policy or advantage of [immigration] taking place in a body (I mean the settling of them in a body) may be much questioned; for, by so doing, they retain the language, habits, and principles (good or bad) which they bring with them. Whereas by an intermixture with our people, they, or their descendants, get assimilated to our customs, measures, laws: in a word, soon become one people."[2] Fonte further noted that:

> In a 1790 speech to Congress on the naturalization of immigrants, James Madison stated that America should welcome immigrants who

could assimilate, but exclude those who would not incorporate themselves into our society. Both Thomas Jefferson and Alexander Hamilton saw advantages to immigration, but worried about the assimilation of newcomers, and insisted that civic integration was necessary for the preservation of the American republic. In *Notes on the State of Virginia*, Jefferson worried that a "greater number of emigrants" came from countries with "absolute monarchies," hence he feared: "They will bring with them the principles of government they leave, imbibed in their early youth; or if able to throw them off, it will be in exchange for an unbounded licentiousness, passing, as is usual from one extreme to another. It would be a miracle were they to stop precisely at the point of temperate liberty..."

Alexander Hamilton insisted that: "The safety of a republic depends essentially on the energy of a common national sentiment; on a uniformity of principles and habits; on the exemption of citizens from foreign bias and prejudice; and on the love of country..."

Hamilton opposed granting citizenship immediately to new immigrants: "To admit foreigners indiscriminately to the rights of citizens, the moment they put foot in our country would be nothing less than to admit the Grecian horse into the citadel of our liberty and sovereignty." Instead, Hamilton recommended we should gradually draw newcomers into American life, "to enable aliens to get rid of foreign and acquire American attachments; to learn the principles and imbibe the spirit of our government; and to admit of a philosophy at least, of their feeling a real interest in our affairs."[3]

It is clear what the Founding Fathers had in mind. To become an American citizen meant becoming an American in values, culture, and historic understanding. Citizenship was something to be studied and acquired, not merely a piece of paper to be granted. Furthermore, citizenship was exclusive and required renouncing any other allegiance.

Dual Citizenship Undermines America

One of the most insidious assaults on American exceptionalism has been the rise of dual citizenship in which people no longer have to renounce allegiance to any other government in order to become Americans. This is a clear break with the Founding Fathers and the essence of American uniqueness.

It is part of an ongoing assault on citizenship. In *Perez v. Brownell* (1958), the Supreme Court ruled that Congress could strip Americans of their citizenship if they voted in a foreign election (Justice Felix Frankfurter wrote the majority opinion). Just nine years later, in *Afroyim v. Rusk*, the Court overturned its own precedent by a 5 to 4 margin. The four dissenting justices noted this discrepancy in a dissent written by Justice John Harlan:

> The court today overrules *Perez*, and declares SEC 401(E) unconstitutional, by a remarkable process of circumlocution. First, the court fails almost entirely to dispute the reasoning in *Perez*; It is essentially content with the conclusory and quite unsubstantiated assertion that Congress is without "any general power, express or implied," to expatriate a citizen "without his assent"... I can find nothing in this extraordinary series of circumventions which permits, still less compels, the imposition of this constitutional constraint upon the authority of Congress. I must respectfully dissent. There is no need here to rehearse Mr. Justice Frankfurter's

opinion, for the court in *Perez*; it then proved and still proves to my satisfaction that SEC 401 (E) is within the power of Congress.

The Supreme Court has been encroaching in an area where congressional intent has been very clear for more than two hundred years. Congress insisted on a renunciation of prior allegiance in 1795. The oath adopted then asserted: "I do solemnly swear... to renounce and abjure absolutely and entirely all allegiance and fidelity to any foreign prince, potentate, state, or sovereignty." It was very clear to the Founders that allowing dual allegiance would subject the United States to a substantial threat of being infiltrated and manipulated by people who were not patriotic Americans.

The dangers of dual citizenship are illustrated by Harvard professor Samuel Huntington. "In 1998, a Mexican law took effect that permitted Mexican immigrants to retain their Mexican nationality while becoming U.S. citizens. 'You're Mexicans—Mexicans who live north of the border,' President Zedillo told Mexican-Americans." Huntington notes, "in 1997 a city councilor in Hackensack, New Jersey, ran for the Colombian Senate and if he had been elected planned to hold both offices simultaneously."[4]

Huntington warns that "with dual citizenship, American identity is no longer distinctive and exceptional. American citizenship becomes simply another add-on to another citizenship."[5] He goes on to argue that "the concept of dual citizenship is foreign to the American Constitution." According to the Fourteenth Amendment, "All persons born or naturalized in the United States, and subject to the jurisdiction thereof, are citizens of the United States and of the State wherein they reside..."[6] Today, by federal *regulation*, immigrants, in their oath of allegiance, renounce all foreign loyalties. I support the Alexander-Ryan bill (S 1628) that would make this a matter of prosecutable federal *law.*

Making Citizens

We need a massive effort to teach immigrants and their families American history and American values. Eighty-eight percent of Americans agree that "schools should make a special effort to teach new immigrants about American values."[7] Americans feel so strongly about teaching America's language and culture to new immigrants that 65 percent believe schools should help immigrants learn America's language and culture even if it means their native culture is neglected.[8] When asked "what should be the bigger priority: teaching students to be proud of being part of this country and learning the rights and responsibilities of citizenship, or focusing on instilling pride in their ethnic group's identity and heritage," 79 percent of parents chose pride and learning in America.[9]

Similarly, foreign-born parents know how important it is for their children to learn about their new country. In the same Public Agenda 2000 survey, 80 percent of Hispanic parents chose pride and learning about America and 73 percent of foreign-born parents preferred America to their country of origin. Even in the least supportive community, African Americans, 66 percent favored their children learning about America and only 29 percent preferred learning about their heritage.

At the federal and state level, we can take a number of steps to encourage the teaching of American history to immigrants. The U.S. Department of Education should cooperate with state governments to create on-line American studies programs in every major city. The Office of Migrant Education should have an American studies program and every English language instruction course should be required by federal law to base such instruction on patriotic American history.

English as a Primary Language

English is not, and never has been, the only language in America. Benjamin Franklin worried about German immigrants and their German language newspapers. There has been a long tradition of people speaking many languages in their local community and with other immigrants. English has been and should remain the primary language of America.

Americans instinctively know that English matters—81 percent believe immigrants should learn English.[10] Far from listening to the American people, the liberal establishment has done everything it can to diminish the importance of English and to promote bilingual education. We cannot let liberals divide the country this way. One proposal to accelerate English fluency is to create a National Program for English Instruction. The program would be modeled after the highly successful "Ulpan Studies" program in Israel. Congressman Chris Cox of California describes the program in a bill he introduced in Congress:

> Immigration policy is a quintessentially federal function. Given the importance of acquiring English language skills, and the lack of a federal policy to address the English language deficiency that many of our new immigrants face, the House Policy Committee has been reviewing ways to encourage English-language acquisition by new immigrants.
>
> In 2003, the Policy Committee met with the leaders of the Jewish Agency for Israel, which administers the Ulpan program—a program of intensive Hebrew language training provided to new Israeli immigrants from around the world. Like the United States, Israel has a polyglot immigrant mix, including Eastern Europeans, Central Asians and Ethiopians, most of whom speak little or no English. Every new immi-

grant to Israel is entitled to 500 hours of intensive Hebrew language training, which is designed to give them the language and practical skills to participate in everyday Israeli life. Although the program is not compulsory, participants receive a small stipend to defray expenses and receive a certificate upon successful completion of the program. This certificate has real value, since many employers require an "Ulpan certificate" for a job and many schools require one for admission.

The Ulpan Studies Authorization (USA) Act will create an equivalent program for new legal immigrants in the United States. Under the USA Act, new legal immigrants will be entitled to intensive English language and civics training—with English language immersion instruction, training in American history and government, as well as in practical skills necessary for seeking employment. Like the Israeli system, the USA Act will provide 500 hours of intensive instruction over five months. To encourage participation, the program will provide a small stipend to help defray the new immigrant's expenses. As a further inducement, the program will provide certain benefits—including shortening the naturalization period by one year—for applicants who successfully complete the course and who pass a rigorous final exam that tests English language proficiency and knowledge of American history and government.

Chris Cox's proposal is the kind of innovative solution that is a "win-win" for new immigrants and the future of America.

For more information on patriotic immigration,
visit **www.newt.org/winningthefuture**

Chapter 6

Patriotic Education

Our own children—not just immigrants—need a patriotic education which today is denied them by an entrenched education bureaucracy. We cannot win this fight *within* the education establishment; we need to break out of the establishment so that we can bring pride and patriotism back to our schools.

First, the House and Senate education committees—and the education committees of each state legislature—should establish standing subcommittees on patriotic education. These subcommittees should give school boards and parents standards by which patriotic education will be taught. Failure of schools to meet these standards would result in an end to federal and state funding.

Second, the U.S. Department of Education—and all state departments of education—should establish a program office in patriotic education. We need new curricula and new textbooks including elementary school books that combine learning to read with patriotic stories.

Third, the Library of Congress should be asked to develop, as part of its digital library, a resource system in American history for teachers, parents (including home-schoolers), and students. By placing this material on the Internet, the Library of Congress can give every student and teacher—even in the smallest and poorest schools—a world-class resource. The Library's on-line version of "Religion and the Founding of the American Republic" is an excellent model.

Fourth, the National Endowment for the Humanities should be asked to promote patriotic education and culture by sponsoring conferences on exploring and understanding American history. They should also host conferences and sponsor publications on integrating new immigrants into the American experience and encouraging the study of American history.

Fifth, the Corporation for Public Broadcasting should be asked to organize its extensive library of patriotic programs so teachers have rental access to every PBS series on American history.

Sixth, state legislatures should require schools and undergraduate programs at state universities to have an American history curriculum for all students.

Seventh, I encourage the alumni and trustees of private colleges and universities to organize committees for American education. They should insist that their schools require courses be taught without the usual extreme leftist bias of most professors, and that every one of their students graduates with a firm grounding in American history.

With these proposals, we can ensure that America's rich heritage and history will be passed on to future generations of Americans.

For more information on patriotic education,
visit **www.newt.org/winningthefuture**

Chapter 7

Patriotic Stewardship

There are Americans who find it very difficult to fully participate in the rights that God has endowed them. Many of these Americans find themselves in this situation through no fault of their own. They were born into shattered communities. They had no one in their family with a work ethic. They had no one nearby to serve as a role model or mentor. There are also Americans who are born with physical or mental challenges. We have an obligation to help our fellow citizens: the poor, the disabled, the deprived. We can think of this obligation as patriotic stewardship.

When President George W. Bush spoke of compassionate conservatism, he was getting at this same point. And it was author Marvin Olasky, the most important student of American charity, who, in his book *The Tragedy of American Compassion,* showed that while the welfare state perpetuates poverty, private charitable efforts—most often faith-based—have been truly effective at helping people.

There's a reason for this.

As former Congressman J.C. Watts notes, people must learn that there is a direct relationship between effort and reward. A good example is the Rescue Mission, a national, non-profit, faith-based organization that helps the homeless after they commit to a program of self-help. Indeed, the Rescue Mission leaders believe it is absolutely destructive to subsidize the problems of poor and addicted people. They need to be taught the values and discipline to overcome them.

Faith has always been a major component of improvement. A senior federal bureaucrat once told a friend of mine that "we know Alcoholics Anonymous is the most effective recovery program in the world. If you could drop the first step (belief in a higher being), we could provide federal funding for the other eleven steps." But it's the first step that's the most important. Alcoholics and drug addicts are often only saved by faith-based programs. Faith provides hope, guidance, and self-discipline while bureaucratization and welfare encourages passivity and undermines and embitters people—their lives reduced to dependent status with no future and no hope.

The bureaucracy actually keeps score in terms of maintaining rather than improving people. There are no rewards for getting people off federal programs and no rewards for getting people back into the community with full-time jobs and independent lives.

It has been forty years since President Lyndon Johnson declared a "war on poverty," yet many of our poorest neighborhoods today are more violent and drug-infested than they were then. We need to learn the obvious lesson that the welfare state doesn't work.

Our first goal should be to establish hope for every American. President George W. Bush's language is right: "no child left behind." And the way to ensure that is to provide a phone number as universal as 911 so that even young children know they have somewhere they can turn to and who can direct them to a faith-based organization that can help. Our goal should be to say to every American who needs help: "If you decide to change your life, your fellow citizens are here to help you. You have to make the first call and you will have to change but we will do all we can to make that change a success so you can enjoy all the blessings of being American." We can do no less if we truly want to be patriotic stewards. And it is not just the poor, the abused, and the addicted that we need to help, it is the disabled who are too often warehoused and offered a minimal quality of life and no hope for the future. Too many government programs for the disabled are run for the convenience of bureaucrats—for example, denying benefits to disabled people who work and who contribute to society but cannot possibly pay for all their health care needs with their salary. That's simply wrong. Every American has a right to the pursuit of happiness and government should not stand in the way.

Compassionate conservatism also needs to address the outrageous brutality and violence that the drug culture has brought to our cities. In the past, places like Hell's Kitchen in New York were rare. Today virtually every major city has at least one troubled neighborhood characterized by rampant criminal violence and a culture that makes role models of drug dealers and pimps. In areas like this the virtue of self-discipline, neatness, hard work, and education are lost.

No healthy society can tolerate what former Senator Daniel Patrick Moynihan described as "defining deviancy down," which is what we have done by glamorizing gangster rap, sadistic computer games, and the stars of destructive films.

It is time to draw the line between an America we can be proud of and an America we have to be ashamed of.

Patriotic stewardship means we need the same passion and determination to protect other children from crime and deviance as we protect our own children. To make patriotic stewardship effective in our poorest and most violent neighborhoods there are five strategies we must implement.

We must reestablish boundaries for our culture by having the federal government use its power over the public airwaves and interstate commerce to crack down on obscenity, indecency, and barbarism. The Federal Communications Commission has started to do this. Much more needs to be done.

We must take young children out of violent homes by enrolling them in prep schools for the poor. When there are drugs in a home it is dangerous to leave an innocent child there. When a mother has boyfriends who are violent it is dangerous to leave a child there. When we have evidence a child has been physically hurt, we should act. We should make the investment to give every child a chance to break out of the cycle of poor education, addiction, and violence. We should support faith-based institutions—like the famous Boys Town—and use them as prep schools for kids in need.

We must make learning profitable for the young by offering direct rewards for poor children who buckle down, do their homework, and learn. There is such a program, the Knowledge is Power Program (KIPP), and it works by giving poor, inner-city kids an incentive to succeed with small cash payments that can be spent at a school store and with the possibility of a trip to Disney World for students who have worked hard all year. I have no doubt that if we give poor children a choice between earning money at school or earning money on the street, many students would avoid the pimps, hustlers, and drug dealers because not only would they be rewarded, but they would see how education leads to a much better future.

We must help the community protect itself by supporting inner-city neighborhood watch groups. We must give every first-time prisoner, except the most violent, rehabilitation from addiction or other problems and vocational training. Parole should be contingent on violent prisoners wearing electronic bracelets for surveillance. We must create a ladder of success for prisoners to rejoin society. Faith-based institutions should be recruited to play a major role in the parole process for every prisoner, especially the young first offenders.

Also, let me be blunt: These problems disproportionately affect African Americans, and we need to recognize that it is harder to be black in America than it is to be European, Asian, or Latin American because of the history of slavery and government-endorsed segregation and welfare dependency. Slavery and segregation are gone. But we have a long way to go to undo the culture of dependency, crime, and deviancy that the welfare state has created and sustained. Compassionate conservatism that embraces all Americans can change this.

For more information on patriotic stewardship,
visit **www.newt.org/winningthefuture**

Chapter 8

A 21st Century Intelligent Health System

I have a very personal interest in better health. I am now sixty-one years old. I am acutely aware of the difference in the quality of life between active, healthy aging and growing steadily more fragile and limited because I fail to take care of myself. I am much more interested in long-term living than in long-term care. And I know that unless I take care of myself, I will either die prematurely or others will end up having to take care of me at great expense.

When I look at my two grandchildren—Maggie and Robert—I know how different their lives will be if they remain physically active instead of becoming obese and acquiring type 2 diabetes, which we used to call "adult onset" diabetes until twelve- and fourteen-year-olds began to get it. The right approach to health will give me a better life as I grow older, and will give Maggie and Robert better lives as they grow up and become adults.

Today, health costs are the largest sector of the economy and it will get bigger as new and expensive breakthroughs in medicine come online and the numbers of aging baby boomers explode. Some studies show health care growing from almost 14 percent of our economy today to 21 percent (or one out of every five dollars) in a few decades.

Without dramatic change, the current system will gradually crowd out more and more spending on other items. Already governors are seeing their Medicaid and state employee health costs eat into education, highways, law enforcement, and other budget priorities. Many businesses now rank health care as their fastest-growing expense and believe that it is a serious burden in competing internationally.

If our country takes the right approach, baby boomers will live longer and better, cost their children less, and create an economic boom for America.

Yet there is also the possibility that we will take the wrong approach. Indeed, the approach favored by much of the news media, many politicians, and liberal government and corporate bureaucracies is the wrong approach.

Virtually every political story about health focuses on "reforms" for our problems: the rising cost of health care, the challenge of the uninsured, the state and federal budget crises, the high cost of drugs, litigation, nursing shortages, doctor unhappiness. The list goes on and on. The truth is that the current health system cannot be reformed because its approach is profoundly wrong in three specific areas. First, it emphasizes acute care rather than wellness, early detection, and prevention. Second, it focuses on third-party payments, an area in which the individual has little responsibility, little knowledge, and no control. And third, it relies on paper (i.e. paper medical records and paper prescriptions) rather than information technology. This has contributed to as many as 98,000 deaths in hospitals due to preventable medical errors.

We need to transform our health care system based on an entirely new set of principles. Our new 21st Century Intelligent Health System will be built around three big changes:

1 Move knowledge from the doctor's office and scientific laboratory to the individual as rapidly as possible;
2 Help the health care system adopt top quality information technology systems to increase productivity, accuracy, and cut costs.
3 Center the process of health on the informed individual so he or she can have the knowledge, desire, responsibility, and opportunity to live the longest life, with the best health, at the lowest cost.

If these three big changes occur, we will live longer, healthier lives and spend less on health care than we do now. This may sound like some fantastic, impossible dream, but I have worked on health care issues for the last six years and I know that this future is possible.

In this chapter, I will discuss the three changes we need to make in order to revolutionize our health care system. Included in this discussion will be the rights Americans should expect in our new 21st Century Intelligent Health System; the responsibilities that should be expected of every American; and the key steps to building this new approach.

The 21st Century Intelligent Health System

To achieve this transformation in health care, we need to:

I. Move from Scientific Knowledge to Personal Solutions

Putting the latest medical science into your bathroom medicine cabinet is today a very slow, cumbersome, and unpredictable process, and because of that people suffer needlessly and die unnecessarily. Consider the case of cancer. Dr. Andy von Eschenbach of the National Cancer

Institute has established a goal of ending cancer as a cause of death by 2015 (go to the NCI website at www.nci.nih.gov for more details).

Yet the National Institute of Medicine reported that it can take up to seventeen years for a new best practice to reach the average doctor. That would mean that success in 2015 might only reach your doctor's office by 2032. How many Americans will have died unnecessarily in the intervening seventeen years?

Dr. von Eschenbach has created a very simple model called DISCOVER-DEVELOP-DELIVER which he believes will solve the problem and save both lives and pain. He argues that if we can rapidly move from the DISCOVER to the DEVELOP phase, that is, move new discoveries from the laboratory to the companies for development, we can turn new knowledge into new solutions at a much more rapid rate. This will require changes in the way scientists report new knowledge. (Today it can take months or even years for a prestigious publication to publish a new ground-breaking discovery.) It will also require the Food and Drug Administration to rethink the time and cost built into the current system. Our current, overly risk-averse system increases the likelihood that you will die before new treatment is approved. Only a bureaucracy could regard that as a success.

Once a product has been DEVELOPED, we have to change the way bureaucracies reimburse health care providers and institutions so the newest technology and therapy can be DELIVERED as rapidly as possible. And the Agency for Health Research and Quality should be charged with ensuring that all information for learning about new drugs and procedures go to doctors and patients.

The DELIVERY phase has to include an Internet-based, real-time continuing medical education system that enables doctors to learn the newest and best solutions. It should include videoconferencing to allow medical professionals to consult and learn in a way that is both cost-effective and saves time. This new delivery system should provide information that is accessible to patients and their families so they can be more involved and knowledgeable about their care.

If we build the DISCOVER-DEVELOP-DELIVER model not just for cancer but for all health care, including mental health, America will rapidly become the most desirable care provider in the world for anyone with a complicated illness.

Lead the World in Health Care

America's health care industry, as the primary provider of health care for the world, will generate the biggest job-creating and prosperity-creating opportunity for the country.

Our health care system will be second to none—a national asset that attracts people around the world to "buy American" services and products to improve their own health. With the right approach, we will be able to offer the newest and the least expensive drugs to Americans and the rest of the world.

Many of our brightest young men and women will go into health care and focus on serving others as a way of life. We will end the emerging epidemic of obesity and diabetes. We may well end cancer as a cause of death and suffering. If we reduce costs, the federal and state budgets will be easier to balance, freeing up more resources to meet other priorities as well as to lower taxes.

To achieve this, we have to take a number of steps beginning with the creation of an undersecretary of commerce for health whose entire job is to focus on protecting America's economic interests in health around the world. This will include stopping the Canadians, French, Chinese, Indians, and others from blackmailing American companies and stealing their intellectual property rights, particularly with respect to drug development.

We also have to encourage the worldwide sharing of information about best outcomes and best practices so every citizen in the world can begin to compare the rationed, obsolete, and inadequate drugs and technology to which their governments restrict them, to the quality of life they could have if only they were allowed to buy American products and services. When Canadians learn it will take months to get a test, they go to Detroit, Buffalo, or Seattle. We need to encourage people from other nations to do the same. One key step in this direction will be to develop very powerful and effective telemedicine and videoconferencing capabilities so people worldwide can access the best American specialists and the newest expert knowledge.

Finally, we have to develop a system of medical tourism in which travel to the United States becomes the standard of care for complicated diseases and newest, best outcomes. Northwestern Hospital in Chicago and the Mayo Clinic in Minnesota have attracted people from all over the world because of the outstanding care they provide. Medical tourism requires a marketing attitude toward health needs worldwide. We must ensure that homeland security visa requirements do not become so difficult and so irritating that people simply refuse to come to the United States even when we provide the best care.

II. Bring Technology and Management Advances to Health Care

Productivity has continued to explode in many of America's industries. But health care has been wrongly insulated from the competition that brings about higher productivity and lower cost. The issue is not that health care is different. In fact, when there is a commercial market in health care, prices behave much as they do in any industry. Everyone has watched the cost of laser eye surgery decline as it has grown more common, more convenient, and safer. Studies have shown that the cost of cosmetic surgery, where people research quality and price, and pay out of their own pockets, has risen slower than the cost of living and in some cases has even decreased. When people are involved and quality and price information are available, people do in fact behave rationally in health care just as they do in purchasing other products and services.

The lesson of nearly four hundred years of entrepreneurial, technology and science-based free market capitalism is very clear. You should expect to get more choices of higher quality at falling prices. This is the opposite of the rationing mentality of some left-wing politicians and the scarcity mentality of too many bureaucrats.

We need to bring these concepts into health and health care. We must insist that doctors, hospitals, medical technologies, and drugs have both quality and cost information available on-line so people can make informed decisions. We can then shift the purchasing decision to the patient and his family so they can make their own cost and quality trade-off decisions.

There should also be an on-line drug purchasing system where patients, doctors, and pharmacists can choose the best product at the best prices, and it should be an after-pay system. Financial incentives could potentially bring down drug prices by 30 to 50 percent from the current marketplace. We should insist that every hospital have computerized order-entry for medication; bar-coding for drugs, technologies, and supplies; and automated medication dispensing.

Indeed, the health system must become paperless. Health information should be made available on-line and in real-time to both providers and patients so they can easily, conveniently, and inexpensively understand their options and their costs. This "right to know" about cost, quality, and outcome should be established in every state.

And we should set a standard that doctors who become paperless get electronic funds transferred every night so they no longer lose money waiting to be paid.

If we insist on modernizing the health system and turning it into an entrepreneurial system with honest reporting of costs and quality, we will rapidly see dramatic changes. Hospitals will start billing based on real costs rather than on stunningly complex cross-subsidies no one understands.

We will also have to develop new models of compensation. A fee-for-transaction model is a bad model because it encourages the doctor to do just enough to bring you back for another transaction to earn another fee. Today we pay for visits and we get billed for visits. With new information systems, we can measure outcomes. When we pay for better outcomes, we will start getting more providers focused on wellness rather than acute care.

The wide-scale availability of information on the best practices and outcomes creates an opportunity to develop a new system of health justice. The need for transformation of our litigation system is outlined in another chapter but it has to be noted that the threat of litigation is a major factor in rising health costs. Malpractice insurance is driving doctors out of their practices. If we do not do something decisive to replace the predatory, personal injury lawyer-enrichment system with a more responsible system of health justice, we will end up as a country with richer and richer lawyers while the rest of us get poorer and poorer health care.

III. Center the Process on the Individual

The biggest single reason health costs keep going up is the third-party payment system, that is, the current insurance system. It is an invitation to conflict, fraud, and frustration. If one person pays, a second person receives, and a third person provides the good or service, what you have is a mess.

A direct buyer-seller system is much healthier. It reduces fraud, corruption, and anxiety. It encourages health care providers to focus on quality, efficiency, and satisfying the patient rather than the insurance company.

All this is changing but it has to be profoundly transformed. We will never have maximum health at minimum cost unless the patient is at the center of the system. Diabetes can only be controlled by the person living with diabetes. The doctor, nurse, and diabetes educator can coach, educate, and encourage, but in the end, people with diabetes must take care of themselves. Similarly, the quality of life for rheumatoid arthritis, such as my daughter Kathy has, is directly a function of the time, energy, and creativity she puts into understanding her own body, her own psychology, and the team she forms with the expert doctor in thinking through a strategy to optimize her quality of life.

We have turned health care into a rental car. No one washes a rental car. Virtually everyone takes better care of their own car or their own house than they do of rentals. If we turn health care back into an area of personal, individual responsibility, we will end up with better health and lower costs.

The following are the three principles that are the foundation for a 21st century health care system:

- Focuses on wellness, early detection, prevention, and maximum quality of life—the individual carries a substantial part of the responsibility for his or her own health care.

- Provides easy access to information about cost, quality, wellness, prevention, and choice through an information technology system available on-line.
- Centers on the individual who has the financial incentives and information to make smart decisions.

Early Success Stories

After the Bush administration ruled in June 2002 that health reimbursement accounts could be carried over from year to year, there were some pioneering companies that experimented with giving individuals both information and incentives. Here is a chart of seven success stories from the first year of health reimbursement account experiments:

CONSUMER CHOICE HEALTH CARE—2003

Company	Budgeted Health Inflation Trend	Actual Health Inflation Trend *(for first year of plan after plan was introduced)*
Equitrac	+15%	-45%
Company S	+20	-6
Hospital System	+15	-31
Trover Health Solutions	+19	-26
Logan Aluminum	—	-18.7
Mercy Health Plan	+16	-9
Wise Business Forms	+10	-13.3

Note: The above are early results and are not necessarily representative of the experience of each company utilizing consumer choice health plans. Year-to-year claim activity will vary and annual results will show more volatility if the population is small. For small employers with slightly higher or lower numbers, large claims will have a significant impact.

The companies shown experienced a drop in health care costs from 6 percent to as much as 45 percent, after projecting 10 to 20 percent increases.[1] The federal government and the private sector should study these enormous breakthroughs. And since Medicaid and state employee health costs combined are the fastest-growing part of every state budget, every governor should have a working group on this new model.

Health Savings Accounts

We can also transform the system with new Health Savings Accounts (HSA) that allow individuals to put their own money in an account tax-free. If you spend the money on health care, prevention, long-term care, or long-term care insurance, it is tax-free when you use it.

The Health Savings Account is personal property so it follows you from job to job during your career. Four out of every five people do not have a major health problem before sixty-five. As a result they could end up with a significant savings account. It's been estimated that an eighteen- or nineteen-year-old who has a Health Savings Account and maintains his health could end up with $250,000 in his account when he reaches age sixty-five.

The power of Health Savings Accounts is multiplied when it is combined with information and prevention. Ralph Korpman of Healthtrio estimates that every American could have an individual health record on the Internet for a $10 start-up fee and could keep it up for about $3 a year. That would mean you could have access 24 hours a day, seven days a week to all the information you need to monitor your own health and to manage any health challenges that are chronic. This new access to accurate information will begin to transform health behavior.

We should have a system of establishing an individual health record for every American and make it a legal responsibility for doctors, hospitals, and laboratories to share the information with the patient.

Wellness and Prevention

The scientists at Nestlé convinced me several years ago that a combination of activity, attitude, and good nutrition, could go a long way in preventing individuals from becoming patients. This principle has certainly proven true in the area of obesity and diabetes. Dr. Dean Ornish has produced dramatic research that indicates these same three areas can have a tremendous impact on heart disease (where he has actually reversed severe heart disease through strict diet, exercise, and meditation), prostate cancer, and other conditions.

As both the Nestlé and the Ornish models suggest, there is a strong connection between mental health and physical health. Lifestyle changes, including increased physical activity, can reduce obesity and related physical ailments, while also decreasing depression and anxiety. An intelligent health system cannot ignore mental health. Statistics indicate that 20 percent of our country's population suffers from mental illness each year, with depression being the most common. Yet less than one-fourth of those diagnosed with depression receive treatment for it. Without treatment, the consequences of mental illness include unnecessary disability, unemployment, substance abuse, homelessness, inappropriate incarceration, and suicide. The cost in human suffering is profound and the economic cost unsustainable.

An intelligent health system would create incentives and information to help prevent avoidable mental illnesses and to help manage existing conditions. For those already suffering from mental illness, it would focus on early diagnosis and treatment to prevent or reduce the severity of future episodes. As with illnesses like diabetes and high blood pressure, early identification and treatment of mental illness would be an important part of the system, resulting in quicker recovery and reduction of harm.

The faster we can make this transition to a system where informed, motivated individuals take care of themselves in partnership with doctors, nurses, coaches, and other health care providers, the faster we will save lives, money, and improve the quality of life of Americans.

All of these changes can be captured in the statement of key rights and responsibilities that characterize our approach to health in the twenty-first century.

IV. Citizenship Responsibility

Your 21st Century Health Rights

1 You have the right not to die from a medical error or a medication error. This right will require individual electronic health records, electronic prescribing, and decision-support systems so doctors and nurses can be guided through the best, newest, most effective knowledge and solutions.

2 You have the right not to be given additional health conditions by the very institutions caring for you. Today there are an estimated 2 million hospital-induced illnesses and 1.5 million nursing home–induced illnesses annually. One in every four people admitted to a hospital contracts an illness they did not have when they entered. That should be totally unacceptable.

3 You have the right to own your own individual health record. Doctors, hospitals, and laboratories could keep a copy of the

information they generate but your health is your property and you should own the record. This will allow you to know what has been done to you, what your current health status is, and what you need to do to maintain the best quality of life and to live the longest life. Your record would be encrypted, and personal privacy would be protected by federal law making it a felony for anyone to misuse your personal health record.

4 You have the right to be part of the lowest-cost insurance pool and you have a responsibility to buy insurance. We need some significant changes to ensure that every American is insured, but we should make clear that a 21st Century Intelligent Health System requires everyone to participate in the insurance system.

People whose income is too low should receive Medicaid vouchers and tax credits to buy insurance. Large risk pools (association health plans are one model) should be established so low-income people can buy insurance as inexpensively as large corporations. Furthermore, it should be possible to buy your health insurance on-line to lower the cost as much as possible.

We should consider allowing people to buy their health insurance from any state that has approved the offer so people are not trapped into plans offered in high-cost states due to the mandated costs passed by their legislatures. People who for libertarian reasons do not want to be insured should be required to post a bond so their health care costs will be covered if they have an accident or an expensive illness.

5 You have the right to know the quality and cost of your doctor, hospital, medical device, drug, or procedure before you make a decision. While it is true that in an emergency, cost and quality

data might be irrelevant, but in most cases people do have time to shop and compare. They should have the information to make that shopping and comparing accurate and convenient.

Every doctor, hospital, and pharmaceutical company should be required to post on the Internet accurate information about price and quality. There is no other aspect of America in which people are asked to choose without knowledge. It is time for health services to offer consumers product and service information that is timely, accurate, and easy to access.

6 You have the right to know your treatment options, including complementary and alternative medicine options, before you make a decision about your course of treatment. Doctors are biased toward what they know. Heart surgeons are more likely to recommend bypass or angioplasty rather than an extreme diet and exercise regimen such as Dr. Dean Ornish has used successfully to reduce heart disease. Some doctors write a prescription for a branded pharmaceutical when a cheaper but possibly equally effective generic or over-the-counter drug is available. In some cases, an experimental treatment or trial may be available that is not yet a mainstream treatment option. It is impossible for doctors to stay current on every new discovery, but modern decision-support systems exist that synthesize the latest medical knowledge pertaining to a particular diagnosis and can be queried to recommend treatment options.

7 You have the right to expect your health provider to have state-of-the-art knowledge about best outcomes. As science produces more breakthroughs in how to solve health problems and as companies develop new technologies and new drugs, the difference

between getting the best and getting the adequate is often going to mean a big difference in quality of life or even between life and death.

Your 21st Century Health Responsibilities

1. Your country should expect you to be engaged in maintaining your own health, looking at your individual health record, and taking responsibility for being aware of your health challenges.
2. Your country should expect you to pay something toward your health care. Even if you are on Medicaid you should pay at least $1 or $2 so that the services you receive have meaning to you. If you have a job and you incur a bill for health care, you have the same obligation to pay it that you would have in buying a car or buying a house.
3. Your country should expect you to make reasonable decisions about cost when you are relying on others to pay for your care. There is no reason to tolerate a system in which people get in the habit of using an $800 emergency room visit for a $40 office problem.

V. The Key to Building a 21st Century Intelligent Health System

The fact is we have already taken significant steps toward a new model of health and health care. In 1996, when I was Speaker, we introduced into Medicare the first key concepts of choice for seniors so they could play a bigger role in their own health and their own quality of life. In 1996 Congressman Denny Hastert led the effort to move away from the third-party payer model by establishing the medical savings account for small businesses and sole proprietors. With leadership from President George W. Bush, Secretary of Health and Human Services Tommy Thompson, Senate Majority Leader Bill Frist, Speaker Denny Hastert, Chairman Bill Thomas, and Chairwoman Nancy Johnson, America has moved closer to our goal of a 21st Century Intelligent Health System.

In 2002, the government ruled that health reimbursement accounts could carry over year to year. In 2003, Health Savings Accounts were enacted into law. In the same year, we established recommendations for early detection, wellness, and health management. In 2004, the Federal Employees Health Benefits Program announced that it will offer an HSA option to federal employees. We also created a National Coordinator for Health Information Technology and assigned Dr. David Brailer to begin developing a comprehensive plan for moving all federal health activities into the information age. Also in 2004, Medicare records started going on-line so every Medicare recipient could begin to access his or her records on line 24 hours a day, 7 days a week.

All this is just the beginning. There are other must-do items.

We should establish safety standards for the health care system. Today you are 2,000 times more likely to die in a hospital from a mistake than in an airplane crash (1 out of every 1,000 patients died due to medical error versus 1 out of every 1,860,491 passengers dying from a plane crash). We should also create a new system of malpractice law that is fair to both doctors and patients.

We should also create a National Security Health Information Technology program that will house a comprehensive database of medical knowledge that would be accessible to doctors and hospitals instantly in case of a biological attack or a pandemic. It would be a dual-use system that in peacetime could save millions of lives and billions of dollars. The Agency for Health Research and Quality estimates that the application of health information technology should save over $100 billion a year.[2]

We should also insist on electronic drug prescriptions to ensure the right medicine is being prescribed. This will prevent delays due to handwriting illegibility and inappropriate medication prescriptions (a large percentage of all prescriptions today require a call back by the pharmacist). Moreover, this would eliminate each year an estimated 2 million adverse drug events, 1.3 million unnecessary office visits, 190,000 unnecessary hospitalizations, and save an estimated $27 billion.

We should abolish mandatory retirement laws as discriminatory and encourage older workers to share their skills as part-time teachers or transition into full-time teaching roles without having to go through more than a single teacher-education class for certification.

For those who would like more information on these proposals, please refer to *Saving Lives and Saving Money*, written by Dana Pavey, Anne Woodbury, and me, or visit www.healthtransformation.net and see what is being done every day at the Center for Health Transformation to create this new 21st Century Intelligent Health System.

For more information on the 21st Century Intelligent Health System, visit **www.newt.org/winningthefuture**

Chapter 9

From Disabilities to Capabilities: Achieving an Active Healthy Life

Today, aging does not necessarily have to mean infirmity, dependence, and decline. Likewise, being disabled does not have to mean a life of government subsidies and dependency. Government needs to think in terms of individual capabilities instead of disabilities. It needs to think in terms of rehabilitation and renewal rather than warehousing that dependency.

We know that medical technology can offer huge opportunities for improving the lives of the disabled and the aged. And we now know that spiritual, mental, and physical health go together. We know that people who are optimistic, active, looking for opportunities and solutions, have spiritual beliefs, and have social ties to other people have much better health outcomes that those who do not. It is one of the outrages of our current system that it fails to integrate the mental, spiritual, and physical aspects of health and that government, with its emphasis on care-taking and client-dependency, often stands in the way. We should be encouraging faith-based programs that work to help the disabled lead active lives.

Two Approaches to Life

I recently visited Sacramento and was struck by two newspaper articles that ran in the same newspaper on the same day. The first story was about disability pension abuse by the California Highway Patrol (CHP).[1] The second story was about an American soldier determined to lead a full life despite a very severe battlefield injury. The contrast could not have been greater.[2] The first story reported that nearly 10 percent of the CHP budget goes to workplace injury complaints, many of them clearly fraudulent. Among the top brass of the CHP, more than 80 percent file for disability pensions. Pensions created to protect officers injured in the line of duty have become a mere entitlement often greater than the recipient's salary and often used while pursuing another career. The article noted that health conditions that qualified for disability included lower back pain, syphilis, and, in one case, an injury sustained when the employee fell off his desk chair! One deputy commissioner had been awarded $39,000 in a medical settlement and a $109,968-a-year pension—half of it tax-free—for "stress." Two years later the same individual was the security director at San Francisco International airport "on the front lines of the war on terrorism" as the job was described.

This is not a disability problem. It is fraud.

The other story was titled "He Lost a Leg But Not the Will to Serve." The story was about a twenty-one-year-old paratrooper named George Perez, who, after losing his leg in Iraq, re-enlisted in the 82nd Airborne Division where he "is determined to prove he's no less of a man." The story recounted his tireless efforts to rebuild his body so he can rejoin his regiment in Afghanistan. To quote this remarkable young man, "I'm not ready to get out yet. I'm not going to let this little injury stop me. . . ."

The two stories caught my eye because I had recently been contacted regarding a former constituent who was struggling to get assistance from the government to allow her to work. The woman, as a result of multiple sclerosis, has no use of her arms and legs. While serving in Congress, my staff and I had intervened to help her get a computer and training on voice recognition software so she could develop skills that might allow her to attain her biggest dream—going to work. Her struggle, which is ongoing, is a testimony to her courage and what I believe is the greatness of the American spirit.

The contrast between a will to live a full life and cheating and depending on others is stunning.

We have to rethink and redesign the public policies we have created for people with disabilities, for workers' compensation, and for long-term living. Policies and systems that made perfect sense in an industrial era make no sense in the information age. The paternalistic solutions of the twentieth century are actually roadblocks to hope and opportunity in the twenty-first century.

We should start with a thorough assessment of the capabilities and requirements of each individual. People should be assessed on their strengths as well as their needs, and the goal of government programs should be to help people lead the fullest possible lives.

We should encourage people to work, to overcome their obstacles, to avoid dependency, and to live on their own rather than in institutions.

This is a profound break with the "paternalistic dependency" method of the industrial age. It will require fundamentally new approaches to what we subsidize, advocate, and regulate. But it will also dramatically improve the lives of Americans with injuries, and disabilities, and who are growing older. It is our moral duty.

For more information on achieving an active, healthy life,
visit **www.newt.org/winningthefuture**

Chapter 10

Fighting for American Interests Within the World Trading System

For the last two decades, the Europeans have looked with scorn upon the American model of free enterprise. Their response to innovation and challenge has been economic isolationism, rule-rigging, and graceful decay. While they know that a welfare state and unionized work rules are expensive and inefficient, they've decided to live with them.

In the United States, there exists a coalition of union leaders who prefer protection over competition; environmental extremists who value nature over the well-being and prosperity of their fellow citizens; and liberal intellectuals who distrust the fluidity and uncertainty of the market and prefer the orderliness of command bureaucracies. This liberal coalition complains about companies' outsourcing jobs while insisting on corporate taxes that encourage companies to go overseas. They prefer that government impose on business obsolete, absurd work rules, even though these raise costs, lower productivity, and make America less competitive in the world market. These liberals believe in expanding regulation even when it fails to meet any cost-benefit test and clearly drives jobs out of the United States. The Left refuses to reform litigation or create a better system of civil justice even though it knows the explosion of lawsuits makes it less desirable to create jobs and invest in the United States.

The challenge to American economic supremacy from 1.3 billion Chinese and more than 1.1 billion Indians is vastly greater than anything we have previously seen. India's embrace of capitalism and China's bizarre combination of Marxist-Leninist government and free market initiatives will create a future where one-fourth of the world's markets will be controlled by these countries. Those who advocate economic isolationism and protectionism are advocating a policy that could help China and India surpass the United States in economic power in our children's or grandchildren's lifetime.

An American Strategy for a More Competitive World

The European Union (EU), the World Trade Organization (WTO), and our other trading partners have been adopting rules that on the surface have environmental, competitive, or other goals but that in reality undercut American companies. Consider the most recent examples:

The Kyoto Protocol

The Kyoto Treaty on Global Warming was an alliance among the European Union, China, India, and various third world nations to establish limits for carbon emissions in the atmosphere. The rules exempted China and India. They also accommodated European interests and energy investments. But America's large forests, which are capable of absorbing significant amounts of carbon, were not factored into the agreement. In order to comply with the treaty, the United States would have to pay a much bigger economic penalty than would the Europeans.

A Rigged Drug-Purchasing System

The European and Japanese drug-purchasing systems are rigged to cheat American companies and to favor local companies. The French government, for example, threatened to steal American patents unless U.S. companies sold drugs to France at very low prices; the French also then agreed to pay higher prices for older, obsolete, generic drugs that are produced by French companies. The result is higher profits for the French companies that do no research and produce old drugs, and lower profits for the American companies that do all the research into new drugs. The same practice holds true for Japan, where hundreds of tiny Japanese companies produce obsolete drugs while the Japanese government tries to minimize the introduction of new and better drugs.

The European and Japanese governments make it illegal for pharmaceutical and medical technology companies to promote products otherwise unavailable in their countries. In effect, Europeans and Japanese are unwittingly forced to accept poorer health and less-effective medicine for the sake of their governments' bureaucracies.

Intellectual Property Theft

The Chinese and Indian governments turn a blind eye to outright theft of patents and production of counterfeit drugs. Intellectual property theft is a major problem for the American pharmaceutical, entertainment, and computer industries and it is something the United States government should be much more vigorous in fighting.

The United States needs to adopt a more aggressive strategy for negotiating with our trading partners on economic rules, international trading agreements, and the environment. We can start with the European Union by establishing a much larger embassy in Brussels, headquarters of the EU. The EU bureaucrats spend years cutting internal deals and lining up EU member countries to support a particular proposal. We need the equivalent of a mini-cabinet in Brussels with virtually every department represented so that we can monitor and be more involved with the EU. Brussels is going to become the third most important city in the world (after Washington and Beijing) and American representation in prestige, numbers, and access should reflect that importance.

The United States government should also make the protection of intellectual property rights a major trade issue and should be prepared to retaliate against countries that steal American goods and services. Today American inventors, entertainers, researchers, and manufacturers are victims of theft, and their government should do more to protect them.

Tax Incentives That Increase Competitiveness

We need to change our tax policies to make American companies more competitive around the world. One example is the tax incentives for corporate headquarters location. There was a significant tax advantage for Daimler to acquire Chrysler but there was a significant disadvantage for Chrysler to acquire Daimler. By remaining blind to the consequences of our tax code, we are favoring market forces that will gradually lead to more takeovers of American companies by foreign firms (e.g. Siemens taking over Westinghouse). The European Union now blocks American mergers even between American companies (e.g., Honeywell and General Electric). If we want the United States to be the multinational headquarters of the world, we are going to have to rewrite our tax laws so that there are no tax disadvantages to an American firm acquiring an overseas competitor. Moreover, we might want to consider creating an incentive for American firms to make acquisitions so the United States becomes the center of executive talent in the world.

The United States is creating millions of jobs while the job market in Europe continues to stagnate. Moreover, the United States has a rising productivity rate that is beginning to pull away from the European Union. America's new jobs have been to a large degree higher paying, cleaner, healthier, and more desirable than the jobs they replaced. The insourcing of new jobs is far greater than the outsourcing we hear so much about in political and news media rhetoric.

Taxes make a big impact on innovation and adaptation. The United States needs a tax code that favors work, savings, investment, productivity, and creative entrepreneurs. We should abolish the death tax permanently so that entrepreneurs, family farmers, and business owners no longer have to fear losing their life's work to the tax collector.

Furthermore, we must eliminate the capital gains tax to encourage investing. Federal Reserve Chairman Alan Greenspan testified that the most economical rate for taxing capital gains is zero because tax-free capital gains will encourage much greater risk-taking and lead to more entrepreneurial behavior. This leads to more prosperity, a bigger economy, and better jobs.

We should create tax incentives that encourage research and development. The 50 percent research and development tax credit should be made permanent and be applied to companies that are willing to take on government's "grand challenges" (for example, the first inhabitable moon base). Investments in new technology and machinery should also be expensed 100 percent in the first year. The present complex code of depreciation makes no sense in a time of rapid change. It is better to encourage overinvestment in new technology and new machinery to keep American workers at the cutting edge of opportunity. Our goal should be to ensure that American workers have newer, better, and more productive equipment than their foreign counterparts.

Investment in new knowledge to expand the human capital available should be 100 percent deductible as long as it is job or profession related. The deduction could be taken by either the company or the individual depending on who made the investment.

These changes would dramatically accelerate America's competitive development, help us lead the world in productivity, and create high-value jobs.

Creating a Union Movement Committed to Competition

America is a better country for the dedication of Samuel Gompers and others who worked to create the union movement. But the union movement as it stands today has become an obstacle to America's economic growth because the union leadership is often resistant to necessary change.

The leadership of the public employees union is the worst. Private sector unions have had to change because of competition. The construction unions have consistently created programs for work force training, apprenticeships, and more opportunities to use new technology and new methods to increase productivity. The auto workers have also had to change because of the pressure of foreign competition. The public employee unions do not face any of these pressures. They want to get as much out of the taxpayer as they can, and they want to avoid job changes for their members as much as possible. They have become the most politically active union in the country. The more they can control the school boards, state legislatures, and congressional delegations, the more they can deliver for their members and game the system to their favor.

Make Political Dues Voluntary

Today union leaders are able to take money from their members and spend it against their beliefs. This is simply wrong. There should be a federal law that forbids unions to force members to pay for political activity. In the *Beck* decision (*Communications Workers of America v. Beck,* 1988), the Supreme Court ruled that no worker can be required to pay political dues against his will. The unions have done everything they can to make it virtually impossible to implement this decision. When the voters in Washington State, for example, had a chance to vote on this proposition in 1992, they voted overwhelmingly against the government employees unions taking money for political purposes. Initiative 134 passed with 72 percent of the vote. When the unions in Washington State had to rely on voluntary contributions, their resources plummeted.

One of my proudest achievements was creating the Thomas system so every American can access the activities of their Congress on-line.

Why shouldn't a similar system exist so union members can find out what happens to their union dues? This is an area where the union leadership has been the most secretive and opposed to accountability. The Department of Labor should insist on open accountability on all union spending. It should be filed within one week on the Internet so any union member can see it. Congress should pass a Union Membership Right to Know Act creating a regulatory authority charged with maintaining accountability.

The "Take It or Leave It" Option

Today it is illegal for management to explain the full range of options to union members. Why shouldn't a worker know that if he chooses a Health Savings Account he will have higher take-home pay? Why can't workers learn that new productivity improvements increase job security and protect their pensions? Why can't workers have a range of benefit selections that are tailored to their needs? The answer is the unions. While the union leaders have a role in negotiating an overall wage benefits package, the individual worker should have the final choice, not the union boss.

Establish a Learning and Training Component for Unemployment Compensation

Last year, states spent $42 billion on unemployment compensation. At the same time, the federal government spent: $16 billion on higher education programs, $3.3 billion (and declining) on all Workforce

Investment Act programs (job training), $1.9 billion on all vocational education programs, and $1.5 billion on Job Corps programs. The industrial era model of unemployment compensation assumed you had a lifetime job and that you only had to wait around for the factory to reopen. In some ways, unemployment compensation became a tax-paid subsidy to cyclical industries so they could close (for example, the auto plants when they had their annual retooling). Now the process of change means that most people will have five or more jobs in their lifetime. Unemployment compensation should move from subsidizing a waiting period to subsidizing a time of preparation. If you are unemployed, America has a high interest in your learning a new job or skill so you can get a better job in the future. You should not be wasting your life waiting passively when you could be using that time to learn. America will be stronger and more competitive when every unemployed American is learning.

Unions should also follow the leadership of the carpenters union in beginning to work toward an individualized lifetime learning commitment that would combine education and apprenticeship to maximize productivity.

Outsourcing

Government employees' unions must accept that outsourcing is a reality of the information age. There is no excuse for requiring the taxpayer to pay more or the citizen to receive less just so the government employees unions can avoid changes. If a government bureaucracy cannot meet the quality and cost challenge of an outsourcing competitor, then it should not get the job. The public employee unions must shift toward developing strategies to prepare their members to compete rather than expend their efforts trying to outlaw competition. Otherwise both the taxpayer and the recipient of government services find themselves cheated and forced to pay more for less than they should.

If we choose to avoid innovation and competition, we will have conceded the future. If we choose to transform the current system, we take charge of America's destiny.

For more information on fighting for America's interests within the world trading system, visit **www.newt.org/winningthefuture**

CHAPTER 11

BALANCING THE FEDERAL BUDGET

BIG GOVERNMENT LIBERALS fear that balancing the budget will mean slashing government programs. Supply-side conservatives fear that balancing the budget is an excuse to raise taxes. National defense conservatives fear that balancing the budget will make it harder to increase spending on defense and intelligence. Many economists think balancing the budget is irrelevant because inflation is a function of monetary policy and not of running deficits or surpluses. They point out that you can run a big deficit (as we have for the last few years) and have very low interest rates if the monetary policy has defeated inflation.

All these arguments are powerful. But balancing the budget isn't a choice, it's a necessity.

WHY BALANCING THE BUDGET MATTERS

I think there are a number of factors that should convince most citizens to demand a balanced budget as a general national policy.

When there is a permanent deficit there is no reason for any politician to say no to any interest group. If government spending is simply an open-ended credit card with no consequences, why not pander to every group and say yes to every request? That is, in fact, how we ended up with the current absurdly bloated, undisciplined federal government. If deficits do not matter and spending is open ended, the most rational strategy for every bureaucracy is to simply ask for more money. If, however, there is a commitment to balancing the budget, then each agency has to find better ways to do things and more innovative ways to get things done. If you want innovation, better outcomes at lower costs, greater productivity, and a spirit of entrepreneurial public management, the balanced budget creates much more pressure for real innovation.

Over time, the requirement to balance the budget leads to a smaller government. Politicians who have to face the voters because they are raising taxes have a much harder sell to make than politicians who can bring home "free" goodies with only some distant deficit to explain. Keeping the lid on spending through a balanced budget was—prior to 1929—a major brake on government spending. I agree with Milton Friedman that it is the size of government that ultimately matters. I also agree with Friedman that if the choice in any one year was a bigger deficit with a smaller government or a smaller deficit with a bigger government, I would always prefer to have the smaller government with a larger deficit. However, as an historian I think the healthiest periods for democracies in peacetime are periods when the political leadership has had to balance the budget and control spending.

Over time a balanced budget allows for lower interest rates and less inflation. I do not doubt that in any one year the deficit is less important in setting interest rates and inflation than is monetary policy. I do doubt very much, however, if the Federal Reserve can sustain a low interest rate policy if the government runs deficits for a long period of time.

I favor a balanced budget, limited government, low taxation, relatively stable inflation (1 to 3 percent), and low interest rates as the best way to promote prosperity.

Balancing the Budget: The Lessons of 1994–1997

When we wrote the first Contract with America we included a provision calling for a constitutional amendment to require a balanced budget in peacetime (with a provision to waive the requirement if there was a war or economic emergency).

In 1995 we passed the constitutional amendment for a balanced budget in the House but it failed by one vote in the Senate. The House Republican leadership decided to act as though the amendment had passed. That spring, the key budget team, John Kasich (Budget Committee), Bob Livingston (Appropriations), Bill Archer (Ways and Means), Tom Bliley (Commerce), Dick Armey (Majority Leader), Tom Delay (Whip), and I agreed that we would balance the budget within seven years.

The Clinton administration fought against balancing the budget but finally surrendered though it ultimately took a period of shutting down the federal government over Christmas 1995 to finally force the Clinton administration to negotiate seriously. The voters apparently agreed because shortly after the budget shutdown, Appropriations chairman Bob Livingston was able to work with Leon Panetta, President Clinton's chief of staff, to enact the first real decline in domestic discretionary spending since 1981 (those two years remain the only years in which domestic spending was cut since World War II). We balanced the budget and we kept our majority. That sounded to me like success.

In addition to domestic discretionary spending, we went to work on a variety of major reforms including reforming welfare, saving Medicare, and cutting taxes. Welfare reform led to a 60 percent decline in the number of people on welfare, cut costs spent on food stamps, public housing, Medicaid, and other programs, and reduced pressures on federal and state spending. Unfortunately, the state governments spent the savings instead of using them to cut taxes. Thus, in the 2000 recession, many states found themselves in a budget crisis.

We capped our success in the summer of 1997 when we forced President Clinton to sign a balanced budget act, which led to four consecutive years of balanced budgets for the first time since the 1920s.

Keys to the Balanced Budgets of Fiscal Years 1998–2001

The balanced budgets resulted from the Republican Congress's deliberate policies of welfare reform, cutting domestic discretionary spending (the first time in fourteen years), reforming Medicare, and cutting taxes.

The non-defense discretionary spending rose at an annual average of 2.3 percent during the four years I was Speaker. By comparison it had risen at more than twice that rate in Clinton's first two years as president and had risen even faster with the Democrat Congress during the four years before Clinton became president.

The effort to balance the budget gave the Federal Reserve confidence that it could continue to lower interest rates without increasing inflation. We were in effect following a tight, deflationary fiscal policy by balancing the budget. This provided breathing room for the Federal Reserve to follow a looser monetary policy. Lower interest rates and tax cuts stimulated economic growth which was a big factor in closing the budget gap. The supply-side theory that lower tax rates and higher economic growth lead to higher revenue from a bigger economy worked exactly as Congressman Jack Kemp and President Ronald Reagan had predicted.

The combination of domestic discretionary spending restraint, structural reform of welfare and Medicare, and tax cuts for economic growth had produced the balanced budgets we had promised. The result was that the United States paid off $401.5 billion in public debt during the four years the budget was balanced.

How to Balance the Budget in the 21st Century

The war with the irreconcilable wing of Islam is going to be a long war, just as the Cold War was a long war. President Eisenhower was adamant that our economic strength was the bedrock of our military strength, and he insisted on frugality in defense as well as non-defense spending because he was determined to avoid massive debt and inflation. Eisenhower was right. A strong economy is the engine that makes it possible for us to do many other things.

The 9/11 attacks, the recession, and our military buildup to fight the war on terror all combined to create the large deficits we have today. But Republicans are also to blame, after all, we've held the purse strings. It's up to Congress and the president to make the tough decisions, to say no to the lobbyists and the special interests, and to take the political heat when it comes to holding the line on pork barrel spending. This will take leadership and sacrifice—from our elected officials and all Americans.

Our goals should be a balanced budget, declining federal debt, lower taxes, low interest rates with stable money, and a rapidly growing economy. We need to develop economic policies to keep the average economic growth rate above 3 percent—including litigation reform, a pro-savings and investing tax policy, a guest worker program for foreign workers, and a regulatory review to eliminate job-killing and economic growth–killing paperwork.

We must transform the health system so people can live longer and healthier lives while taking 20 percent out of the cost of the system. We can achieve this through the efficiencies of information technology, and by the kind of waste reduction and productivity increases that have been common in manufacturing for the last thirty years and in service industries for the last fifteen years. This alone would save more than $1 trillion in federal spending over the next decade. Transforming health is vital because Medicare is a much bigger long-term obligation than Social Security. This is *the* most important single building block to a balanced budget.

We must replace administrative public bureaucracy with entrepreneurial public management to get the kind of improvements in productivity in the public sector that have happened in the private sector. We can do more with less if we do it in a quality system using information technology and modern communications.

We must privatize government agencies including the airports, Amtrak, the Post Office, and the Tennessee Valley Authority. We need to develop partnerships between government and the private sector for those systems that need to remain in government but would benefit from the entrepreneurial drive and additional human and financial resources a private partner can bring to bear. We should outsource remaining activities where possible to get more productive, more modern, and less expensive goods and services.

We must establish a cap on domestic discretionary spending.

We need to create Social Security personal savings accounts to avoid the fiscal disaster that will otherwise result.

With a program like this, we can expect to work our way back to a balanced budget with lower taxes, lower interest rates, and greater economic growth.

For more information on balancing the federal budget,
visit **www.newt.org/winningthefuture**

CHAPTER 12

THE KEY TO 21ST CENTURY SUCCESS: SCIENCE AND TECHNOLOGY

IN 2001, THE HART-RUDMAN Commission on American National Security, a bipartisan group of experienced leaders, concluded that the greatest threat to America is an attack—probably by terrorists—using a weapon of mass destruction on an American city. The Hart-Rudman Commission added that the *second greatest threat to American national security is the failure of math and science education. In fact, in a unanimously approved provision, the Commission said that the failure of math and science education is a greater threat than any conceivable conventional war in the next quarter century.*

What makes the Hart-Rudman Commission warning about math and science education particularly ominous is that it came eighteen years after the Reagan administration published *A Nation at Risk.* Back in April 1983, Americans were warned that the failure in education was becoming a major threat to the nation. As the title implied, America was literally at risk because of the failings of its education system. "Our once unchallenged preeminence in commerce, industry, science, and technological innovation is being overtaken by competitors throughout the world," the report stated. It went on to soberly note that "what was unimaginable a generation ago has begun to occur—others are matching and surpassing our educational attainments."[1]

For over a century, it has been the knowledge of scientists and technologists, brought to the marketplace by entrepreneurs in the form of products and services, that has driven the pace of progress. Those countries that have adapted to the opportunities created by science and technology have flourished. Those that have ignored them have fallen behind in standards of living and quality of life.

The central role of science and technology will be even greater in this century. We are in the early stages of a revolution in knowledge that will transform the way we live, learn, and do business.

The Science Revolution

It is very hard to predict specific breakthroughs, but relatively easy to foresee general patterns. That is why Jules Verne and H.G. Wells were so interesting to their generation. That is why Alvin and Heidi Toffler's two books, *Future Shock* and *The Third Wave,* were so useful. That is why J.C.R. Licklider was able to be so prescient in describing computing in 1959. We are still, forty-five years later, only partway to Licklider's dream. But with each passing year, his understanding of the human-machine-knowledge interaction becomes more impressive and more perceptive.

I began studying Licklider and the future of computing with Pete Jensen at Georgia Tech in 1965. I also began working with Alvin and Heidi Toffler in the early 1970s. Their ability to see broad patterns has been one of the most interesting aspects of my work for the last forty years.

When you look at the scale of change that is coming in science and technology and combine it with the rise of massive new centers of production in China, India, and elsewhere, you're in a world transformed. Consider the period between 1903 and 2003.

It was in 1903 that the Wright brothers flew for the first time. Their initial flight at Kitty Hawk was shorter than the wingspan of a Boeing 747. It was slow enough for one brother to run with the plane to help keep the wing from tipping over. It was also in 1903 when an American film produced the first cinematic story: *The Great Train Robbery* is still shown at Disney World. It runs about twelve minutes, is silent, and in black and white. It was in 1908 when Henry Ford built his mass-produced car. Ford's achievement of standardized parts (the necessary precursor to the assembly line) revolutionized all of modern manufacturing and is the basis of today's dramatically more productive and, therefore, wealthier society.

Imagine the scale of change from a pre-airplane, pre-motion picture, pre-mass–produced car world, to our world. Then imagine the same approximate scale of change between now and 2030. Our achievements in science, technology, and economic growth will disappear if we fail to invest in science and if we fail to transform our system of math and science education.

Competing in Science

Keeping America competitive in the twenty-first century will be an enormous challenge. Americans have been spoiled by three surprising aspects of the twentieth century that have led us to have an artificially high proportion of the world's best scientists.

First, the Nazis drove a generation of world-class scientists out of Europe. Albert Einstein, Edward Teller, Niels Bohr, and thousands of talented, well-trained scientists and talented future scientists came to the United States in flight from the Nazi monsters who were destroying freedom in Europe.

Second, the communists drove another generation of scientists out of Europe, notably talented mathematicians from Eastern Europe. German scientists like Wernher von Braun played indispensable roles in developing the American missile and space programs. In dozens of fields, European scientists provided a level of talent and knowledge that accelerated American leadership.

Third, the combination of war, political instability, and poverty in the third world led many of the brightest students on the planet to come to the United States for their graduate education and their subsequent careers. By the late 1990s, American graduate programs filled many of their slots with foreign students. In some areas, well over half of the graduate students came from outside the United States. This reliance on foreign-born mathematicians and scientists has worked for a while, but it is unlikely to work in the twenty-first century as other countries invest in their own graduate universities in math and science and improve their economies.

If the influx of foreign students drops off as dramatically as anticipated, the ability of American graduate schools to attract young talent will shrink. And if we do not develop a strategy for maintaining our leadership in math and science, it will be impossible for us to maintain our leadership in national security, economics, and standard of living.

For the last twenty years, we have tried to improve education while accepting the fundamental principles of a failed system guarded by education bureaucrats and teachers unions. We need bold changes or our schools will fail us. The following are highlights of my proposals to dramatically improve math and science education in the United States.

We should set as a goal eliminating 50 percent of the education bureaucracy outside the classroom and the laboratory and dedicate the savings to financing the improvement in math and science education. There has been a steady growth in the amount of money spent on red tape, bureaucracy, and supervision. We now have curriculum specialists who consult curriculum consultants who work with curriculum supervisors who manage curriculum department heads who occasionally actually meet with teachers. The more we have spent on education, the smaller the share we have spent on inspiring and rewarding those doing the educating.

Scientists, engineers, mathematicians, and others who have mastered a subject matter should be allowed to teach after only one course on the fundamentals of teaching. According to a report by the Council of Chief State School Officers in 2003, roughly 30 percent of math and science teachers do not hold a major, minor, or regular certification in their field.[2] The instant students and graduates with majors in math and science know they will be allowed to teach (with appropriate compensation) without having to go through the numerous, boring, and pointless teacher's education and certification courses, we will have a dramatic increase in the number of people who can actually teach math and science.

Moreover, teacher specialists should be allowed to teach part-time so that professionals in their fields can share their knowledge and experience in the classroom. The teachers' union will scream because it will reduce their dues, but the students will have informed, enthusiastic, confident teachers guiding them in difficult subjects. Every state should pass a law establishing an absolute preference for part-time specialists with real knowledge over full-time teachers who do not know the subject. By the 2008 school year, no one should be allowed to teach math and science who is not competent in the subject matter.

We should experiment with paying students for taking difficult subjects. The potential for changing student behaviors and values is especially great in poor neighborhoods where there is no parental support for learning. Today, young people can make money working after school. Some make money selling drugs or selling their bodies. Some seek to make money by being athletes or musicians. In this world of immediate gratification, the long, difficult road to becoming a Ph.D. in math or chemistry has virtually no support in poor neighborhoods. If as early as the seventh grade there were some modest economic reward for learning math and science (say matching twenty hours a week at a McDonald's), the signal sent would be immediate and dramatic. If the rewards went up as the classes grew more difficult we would have students pouring into math and science instead of fleeing it.

As a Congressman, I invented a program called "Earning by Learning." I gave my speech money to pay poor children in public housing $2 a book for every book they read in the summer. The first year, a young girl in Villa Rica, Georgia, read eighty-three books and earned $166. That was big money for a fourth grader in Villa Rica public housing. That fall, she got into trouble when she went back to school because she was too used to reading and kept doing more than the curriculum permitted. She wanted to learn so much that she was considered a troublemaker. Everywhere we tried "Earning by Learning" it worked.

Graduates willing to stay in math, science, and engineering should pay zero interest on their student loans until their incomes reach four times the national average income. The goal would be to encourage math, science, and engineering students to stay in their fields and continue to pursue knowledge.

As NASA develops its aggressive new programs for returning to the Moon and going on to Mars, a series of "research and learning" projects should be developed in which students could be directly engaged in real science at the cutting edge from their classroom. The NASA program of "explorers in school" is already having a big impact on the schools that are taking part. Ultimately, every school in the country should be able to participate in real research. The same principles should be extended to oceanographic and other government research centers.

These ideas are designed to stimulate thinking beyond the timid "let's do more of the same" that has greeted every call for rethinking math and science education since 1983. If the future and safety of our country really are at stake in the areas of math, science, and engineering (and I believe they really are), then we can do no less than respond with an appropriate intensity and scale. But there is much more that must be done if we are to compete in the world market and win.

Scanning Worldwide for New Knowledge

As more of the world engages in science, there will be more new knowledge created outside the United States. This is not a new phenomenon. Prior to 1500, China was the center of scientific knowledge in the world. From around 1500 to 1940, Europe was the center. The United States has only been the center of scientific endeavor for the last sixty years. As noted earlier, much of that success can be attributed to foreign scientists and foreign students coming to the United States. If we want to remain at the forefront of scientific understanding, we have to make a much greater investment in knowing what is being studied and learned around the world.

At a minimum, we need a virtual real-time translation service for every significant language so that scientific knowledge can be made available on-line in the United States without regard to where it was developed or where it was published. We need the equivalent of a Google for science in which American scientists can scan all the developments in their field worldwide. No publication should go more than ninety days without being translated into English. This principle should also apply to the proceedings of international scientific conferences. As rapidly as they are announced, we need to ensure that American scientists are aware of all scientific breakthroughs from around the world.

We should also encourage more foreign scholars to work in the United States in visiting scholar programs. We should increase sabbatical programs for American scientists to work in foreign laboratories and institutions. The amount of knowledge that will be brought back to the United States is incalculable. Historically, we have understood this principle for graduate students and young researchers (American James Watson helped discover the double helix for DNA at Cambridge) but we have not integrated it into the academic career track, budgetary calculations, and management reward systems for more senior people.

Attracting Foreign Students and Researchers

There is a great danger that homeland security considerations will create a visa system so complex and intimidating that foreign students will simply stop coming to the United States. There is considerable evidence that foreign students are already finding it too burdensome and are going elsewhere. As foreign universities and laboratories continue to improve, American universities might be put at an even greater competitive disadvantage.

Americans do not appreciate how much self-inflicted damage is being done by the visa process. The European Union is moving toward a world in which people from twenty-five countries will cross borders without having to show a passport or stop at the immigration desk. At the very time Europe is becoming more open to travel, the United States is building a wall of red tape and intimidation.

I am very much for using biometrics to track terrorists or potential terrorists and for implementing those capabilities as soon as possible. But I am against cutting America off from foreign scientists, students, tourists, and business travelers in the process. We should have a much simpler visa process. For certified students and researchers, the visa work should be on-line and not very time consuming. We must rethink our funding of foreign students and researchers, our documentation program, and our attitude about them. If America ceases to be attractive to world-class talent from all over the world, it is America that will be the loser.

Participation in Worldwide Forums

Recently there has been a dramatic reduction in the number of American scientists who travel to international conferences. This is an example of saving little money at great long-term expense. This is a profoundly self-destructive policy.

American scientists need the knowledge gathered at conferences and the human interaction and stimulation that comes from these meetings. Reading reports and studying conference papers are not a substitute for mingling with smart people from other countries. Back in the 1970s while teaching at West Georgia College, I came across a study of the power of ideas generated from academic discussions and formal panels. The main thesis proposed was that the ideas of the next five years are in private cocktail party discussions while the ideas of five years ago are being presented on the dais at the formal session.

There should be significant investments in foreign travel and in international conferences for American scientists. When in doubt, send more and stay longer. The long-term payoff will be enormous.

Investing in Scientific Research

The research budget of the United States should be considered part of the national security budget. Investing in science (including math and science education) is the most important strategic investment we make in continued American leadership economically and militarily. Investing in science has also been the most consistent, powerful, single mechanism for extending life and for improving the quality of life. When developing the federal budget, the investment in science should be considered immediately after operational military requirements and before any of the traditional domestic spending programs.

Congress should consider establishing a separate budget line item for federal research and protecting it from encroachment by all the interest groups who want immediate gratification for their projects. Special interests can find funding for highways, subsidies to farmers, and public housing. For a variety of reasons scientists and those who believe in science have a harder time making a "pork barrel" or special interest appeal for more money.

In the next few years the requirements are pretty straightforward.

The National Institutes of Health (NIH) should increase at a rate that allows it to sustain its current research program. Having recently doubled the NIH budget, Congress does not need to double it again immediately. Congress should be aware, however, of the crippling impact of a flat budget when research opportunities and needs are growing.

The National Science Foundation's (NSF) budget should be tripled over the next five years. The foundation is the engine of basic research for the United States, and most of our modern medical advances have come as the result of basic research initially funded by the NSF.

The specialized agencies, the laboratories at the Department of Energy, the National Institute of Standards and Technology, and the National Oceanic and Atmospheric Administration should all be asked to develop a master plan for the science they could do if properly funded. Funding should follow proportionate to the research they can explain and defend.

The Department of Energy has an opportunity to transform the entire energy economy (and the American balance of trade) through its work on hydrogen. If the Department of Energy succeeds in developing a commercially sustainable hydrogen market, its impact on the environment, the economy, and national security will be extraordinary. This project deserves as big an investment as it can reasonably use.

The National Institute of Standards and Technology has been leading the way in researching quantum mechanics and its work needs to be continued.

The National Oceanic and Atmospheric Administration has enormous opportunities in ocean science and in understanding global climate change. A society that may end up spending trillions to avoid global climate change should be willing to spend 1 percent as much understanding the topic.

The yardstick should be very simple: What are our children's future and our grandchildren's future worth to us? What are the breakthroughs that might accelerate our economy, save our lives, and protect our nation worth to us? From that baseline we should develop our research budget each year.

Adopting Breakthroughs Whether Home Grown or Imported

New developments achieve their impact when they are adopted in the marketplace or by the right government agencies. The first home computer built at the Xerox PARC laboratory in Palo Alto was interesting but its real power only became apparent a decade later when Steve Jobs translated it into the commercially successful Apple computer. The real power of the Internet reached beyond the technology community when firms like Netscape and AOL began to popularize and commercialize it for the consumer.

There are a series of steps in tax, regulatory, and trade policy that will accelerate this commercialization. Here I want to note that all the government labs should adopt early licensing and royalties programs, have some opportunity for government scientists and engineers to personally profit from these revenues, and the remaining revenue should go back into scientific research and development rather than into the general treasury.

Allowing government scientists to earn some portion from their new ideas and products will increase the desire of first class scientists to stay in the government (which today finds it increasingly difficult to compete with the private sector in salary and benefits). The personal and institutional payoff for research will also dramatically increase the awareness of the need to commercialize and move ideas from laboratory to market. Many universities already have model programs and the federal government should adopt a similar approach.

Transforming America So We Can Compete with Anyone, Anywhere

For the first time since we surpassed Great Britain around 1840, America is facing a serious challenge to our economic superiority. For the last 150 years we have been the most dynamic economy in the world. While Germany and Japan could challenge us in some areas, they were simply not big enough to compete with America in everything.

Now we are faced, in China and India, with countries whose populations are larger than our own. Americans will have to be four times as productive as Indians and Chinese just to match them in overall economic activity (since there will be four times as many Chinese or Indians as Americans). Historically, we have achieved far more than this level of productivity advantage. But as other countries study us and learn what we do, they will learn to be better competitors.

The Japanese were the first great Asian implementers of Western economic productivity.

When Edwards Deming, the father of the quality movement, went to Japan in 1950 to teach a four-day course on quality and productivity, he had little notion that 75 percent of the industrial capital in Japan would participate in the workshop. He also had no idea they would be so impressed by his message that they would name the prize for the best run company in Japan the Deming Award.

Today the Toyota Production System is the foremost example of Deming's teaching.

In the 1980s Japan ran the United States a very serious race in productivity. Even today, after two decades of improvement, American industry has a hard time matching Toyota in productivity.

When Margaret Thatcher ran for prime minister in 1979 she had a commercial that showed a group of runners in a track race. The runner wearing the British uniform was shackled by higher taxes, union work rules, and government regulations. He lost. Margaret Thatcher helped take the shackles off British companies and entrepreneurs.

Former Israeli prime minister (and now finance minister) Benjamin Netanyahu describes his experience in basic training in words that exactly parallel the Thatcher commercial. The Israeli army has a test called "the elephant walk." Each man has to pick up the person next to him and carry that person as far as he can. Netanyahu notes that if a big person has to pick up a small person, the elephant walk isn't very difficult. On the other hand, if the small person has to pick up the big person, the smaller carrier collapses in just a few steps. Netanyahu makes the case that when a country has a big and rapidly growing private sector, it can afford to carry public services without much trouble. But if it has a small, unhealthy private sector, the cost of public services may crush the economy. We Americans should take note of the Thatcher-Netanyahu model and look at the transformations we need in America if we are to successfully compete with China and India in another generation

If we can build on the breakthroughs in math and science described earlier, then our grandchildren will almost certainly live in the most competitive, prosperous, and safest nation in the world. There is an enormous amount of work to be done, but it is a challenge worth meeting.

SPACE: THE REGULATED, BUREAUCRATIC FRONTIER

Space has drifted from being an extraordinary adventure into an endless, underfunded, bureaucratic activity of great interest to scientists and limited interest to entrepreneurs. There is no better example in the need for entrepreneurial public management than the current space program.

President George W. Bush has laid out bold plans for a new dynamic vision of human adventure in space, including going back to the moon and to Mars. But there is almost no hope it can be achieved within the projected budgets. The shuttle and the space station absorb the largest part of the NASA budget; they represent obsolete technologies and limited opportunities for progress. NASA has an additional burden that would have destroyed aviation in its infancy because it requires a safety standard that makes space flight stunningly expensive. People who climb mountains can't meet the NASA standard for safety.

If President Bush attempts to achieve his big goals through a tired system he will never have the money to succeed. Space is now caught in a destructive circle in which Congress refuses to vote the money needed for big missions because it does not trust the NASA bureaucracy and NASA can't do the jobs it is assigned because Congress refuses to fund it. NASA is also elitist. The standard for an astronaut has been set so high that most people know it is not a program for them. Occasionally someone like Jake Garn or John Glenn (both Senators) get to go into space. In Glenn's case he proved that a seventy-seven-year-old could fly into space. But the program is still stunningly restrictive and limited.

Ironically the Russians, in desperate search of hard currency, have become the first country to open up their program to a paying customer, and for $20 million they flew an American millionaire into space. Richard Branson, the founder of Virgin Airlines, and a number of other successful companies have signed contracts to begin taking people into suborbital space as a profit-making venture. He represents the beginning of the real future of the space program. Space will explode with activity as soon as we make a few midcourse corrections.

We should recognize that cost is holding us back. To save taxpayer dollars and energize the private sector, we should offer tax-free earnings for the first twenty-five years of any profits made in space. We should also establish a series of tax-free prizes: a prize for the company that can produce an orbital vehicle at a certain cost; a prize for the first permanent moon base; a prize for breakthroughs in robotics; and so on.

We should establish a system for private trips into space with safety standards equal to climbing Mount Everest—a standard that will dramatically lower costs.

These are just a few of the steps we need to take to rediscover the excitement generated by President Kennedy, and the potential we saw a generation ago, before our space program was smothered in government bureaucracy, caution, and red tape.

For more information on science, technology, and space policies, visit **www.newt.org/winningthefuture**

CHAPTER 13

ENVIRONMENT AND ENERGY: THE FRONTIERS OF OPPORTUNITY

AMERICA WILL BE stronger if it develops coherent technology and market-oriented solutions to environmental conservation and energy consumption. Consider how much better we can do in each field.

It is possible to have a healthy environment and a healthy economy. It is possible to build incentives for a cleaner future. It is possible to have biodiversity and wealthy human beings on the same planet. And it is possible to have free markets, scientific and technological advances, and an even more positive environmental outcome. There is every reason to be optimistic that if we develop smart environmental and biodiversity policies our children and grandchildren will experience an even more pleasant world.

Indeed I believe this is part of every American's stewardship obligation. As the Bible says: God instructed man to "replenish the earth" (Genesis 1:28).

My childhood was surrounded by the natural world. My family had a cabin in the mountains of central Pennsylvania, just below State College. My uncles subscribed to the *Pennsylvania Game and Fish Commission Magazine*. They believed in conserving the outdoors so that as hunters and fishermen they could enjoy the bountiful fruits of nature.

I spent much of my childhood on farms and wandering around the woods and streams of central Pennsylvania. When my father joined the Army I continued my outdoors experience at Fort Riley, Kansas.

When I was a child, Republicans had a strong memory of Theodore Roosevelt as the great outdoorsman and conservationist and Pennsylvanian Gifford Pinchot as the aggressive and bold advocate of national forests. I wanted to be either a vertebrate paleontologist (probably studying dinosaurs) or a zoo director. In either case I wanted to study life and the way it evolved on the planet.

I taught in the second Earth Day at West Georgia College in 1971 and I soon found myself the coordinator of environmental studies teaching courses about the natural world and taking students to the Okefenokee Swamp.

When I first ran for Congress I was the natural candidate of most environmental groups including friends in the Georgia Conservancy, and I was very supportive of conserving natural resources (including the Flynt River in Middle Georgia).

In Washington I soon discovered there is almost no space for a creative, entrepreneurial, science and technology-oriented environmentalism. Instead, Washington was divided between leftists who thought only of regulation, litigation, and blocking development (whatever its benefits to people) and those on the Right who, unfortunately, never factored environmental considerations in their thinking at all.

As Speaker I tried to create a positive approach that recognized both the importance of saving endangered species and the importance of property rights. We developed with Congressman Ralph Regula and the Trust for Public Land a tremendous program for the Chattahoochee

River in Georgia that combined public and private funding to conserve over 130 miles of the Chattahoochee for public use at minimum cost to the federal government and with maximum local involvement.

It is clearly possible to combine human progress with biodiversity. There are more trees in Georgia today than there were in 1900 or 1940. The very increase in wealth in America made it possible in 1895 to found the New York Zoological Society (now the Wildlife Conservation Society) and save the American bison from extinction. The application of new technology and new science has cleaned up the air of most American cities (it is far cleaner now than it was twenty years ago even though people are driving more cars more miles).

The greatest dangers to biodiversity on the planet today are poor people cutting down tropical forests for money and killing endangered species for meat. Wealthy people can afford to protect the forests and protect endangered species.

The greatest areas of pollution and toxic wastes on the planet today are the byproducts of the Soviet Empire and a centralized command bureaucracy that was willing to kill the environment to reach production quotas.

Here are a few examples of the kind of science-based, technologically-oriented environmentalism that could improve our quality of life, increase our options, and enhance the natural world.

We should open up the nuclear waste cleanup program to the best possible technology and the least expensive approaches. This will save years of cleanup and tens of billions of dollars over the current bureaucratic-entrenched approach. There is one privately developed technology that it has been estimated could save twelve years time and $10.6 billion in cost in cleaning up the Hanford facility alone. The money saved could be used for environmental research.

We have made significant progress in cleaning up places like San Francisco Bay and the Chesapeake but there is much more to be done. Some of it can be accomplished by government's tapping innovative private clean-up companies.

We must insist that cities meet their obligations in waste cleanup. Atlanta has been a far larger polluter of the Chattahoochee than any private business, yet the federal government has maintained a double standard between what cities and industries are allowed or required to do. Government should be as responsible for running its waste treatment centers professionally and competently as the private sector. The rivers will be cleaner as a result.

We should encourage the kind of public-private partnerships that have enabled the Trust for Public Land, the state of Georgia, the Robert W. Woodruff Foundation, and the federal government to create environmentally sound land use along the Chattahoochee. It is important for cities, counties, and states to buy parkland when it is cheap and easily available and *before* population growth overwhelms open space. I am a conservative who likes to walk in Central Park in New York and along the Chicago lakefront and along the Chattahoochee recreation area. We can give our children and grandchildren better environments in their lifetimes through reasonable foresight. One step would be to take the Land and Water Conservation Fund off budget so the money can be used as intended and not blocked as a political maneuver to mask the budget deficit.

The world biodiversity hot spots have been identified. These are places where biologists and botanists have discovered unusually rich concentrations of animals and plants. If the United States challenged Europe and Japan to join it in financing a world biodiversity refuge system and tied foreign aid into the process of maintaining biodiversity, we could probably save a very high percentage of the earth's biological richness for our children and grandchildren to enjoy, study, and learn from at a surprisingly small cost (trivial compared to what the Left would spend through the Kyoto Treaty).

Kyoto is a bad treaty. It is bad for the environment and it is bad for America. It sets standards that will require massive investments by the United States but virtually no investments by other countries. The Senate was right when it voted unanimously against the treaty. We should insist on revisiting the entire Kyoto process and resolutely reject efforts to force us into an anti-American, environmentally failed treaty.

The United States should support substantial research into climate science, managing the response to climate change, and in developing new non-carbon energy systems. It is astounding to watch people blithely propose trillions of dollars in spending on a topic on which we have failed to spend modest amounts to better understand. To its credit the Bush administration has begun to increase funding on climate research but much more needs to be done. Furthermore, it is astounding to have people focus myopically on carbon as the sole source of climate change. The world's climate has changed in the past with sudden speed and dramatic impact. Global warming may happen. On the other hand it is possible Europe will experience another ice age. The Norwegian politicians who worry much about global warming (the politically correct thing to do even in a cold country that would demonstrably benefit from a warmer climate) may suddenly find themselves migrating south if a new interim ice age were to happen. This point is politically incorrect but the history and science of climate change is far more complex and uncertain than the politically driven mass hysteria of scientists who sign on to ads about a topic for which they have no scientific proof.

The federal government should establish measurable standards for a healthy environment but allow widespread experimentation in achieving those goals. Too much of the conflict between landowners and federal employees and between cities and states and the federal government are a function of a heavy handed bureaucracy. The lengthy process of environmental planning is made adversarial and expensive beyond reason and should be redesigned to have a collaborative style with the goal of having both development and a healthy environment.

Brownfields (abandoned former industrial sites often with toxic and other wastes that need to be cleaned up) need a new federal law to encourage cities to get them cleaned up. The current system favors litigation over cleanup and has kept thousands of sites in our cities from being cleaned up. The trial lawyers have been winning but the people of the cities have been losing. We need litigation reform and financial encouragement for citizens to clean up the sites. This will help create economic opportunity in our cities, and replace blighted, abandoned areas with new development opportunities.

Ironically many left-wing environmentalists have favored an alliance with trial lawyers even if the current rules encourage businesses to go out and build new factories on green fields rather than rebuild the inner-city sites. This is an area where enormous progress could have been made over the last twenty years if the Left would have recognized that brownfield development was a good thing. But the political alliances of the Left and the trial lawyers have hurt cities, minorities, and the environment in favor of punishing business and enriching the lawyers.

The Bush initiative on healthy forest management is an important step in the right direction. Forests in particular and national lands in general should be run on sound science and conservation principles rather than on emotional rhetoric designed for political effect. The refusal to manage the forests intelligently led to huge beetle infestations in the southwest that produced sicker and poorer forests. The refusal to clear out dead timber across the west led to fires that were hotter, more intense, and therefore more destructive. The left wing of the environmental movement represents a repudiation of eighty years of sound conservation practice that stemmed from the principles laid down by Theodore Roosevelt and Gifford Pinchot. The new healthy forest policies are sound steps in the right direction and should be expanded.

These are just a few examples of how a positive, activist, problem-solving environmentalism could give our children and grandchildren a better world. That goal will be even more rapidly achieved if we make dramatic progress on the energy front.

Energy

A sound American energy policy would focus on four areas: basic research to create a new energy system that has few environmental side effects, incentives for conservation, more renewable resources, and environmentally sound development of fossil fuels. To its credit, the Bush administration has approached energy environmentalism the right way, including using public-private partnerships that balance economic costs and environmental gain.

The Bush administration's investment in developing hydrogen energy resources may be the biggest breakthrough of the next half-century. Hydrogen has the potential to provide energy that has no environmental downside. In one stroke a hydrogen economy would eliminate both air pollution and global warming concerns. Since hydrogen is abundant in the air and water around us, it eliminates both the national security and foreign exchange problems associated with petroleum. Suddenly oil would become a source of petrochemicals and cease to be a source of energy. The relative requirements for oil would shift to making plastics and away from providing fuel. The result would be a lot less reliance on the Middle East and a lot less concern over balance of payments.

A hydrogen economy is probably twenty years away but there seems to be no scientific reason the hydrogen engine cannot be mass-produced. General Motors and virtually every other major automobile manufacturer have major programs underway to develop hydrogen energy designs and production. The potential is real that many of the pollution problems of our lifetime will begin to disappear after 2020 or 2025.

Conservation is the second great opportunity in energy. Already the United States has adjusted to earlier oil price increases by becoming a dramatically more efficient user of energy. But companies like Honeywell and Johnson Controls believe we could achieve 30 to 60 percent improvements in energy conservation if our tax policy better encouraged it and if we set the standard by optimizing energy use in government buildings. A tax credit to subsidize energy efficient cars (including a tax credit for turning in old and heavily polluting cars) is another idea we should support.

Renewable resources are gradually evolving to meet their potential: from wind generator farms to solar power to biomass conversion. Continued tax credits and other advantages for renewable resources are a must.

Finally, it is time for an honest debate about drilling and producing in places like Alaska, our national forests, and off the coast of scenic areas. The Left uses scare tactics from a different era to block environmentally sound production of raw materials. Three standards should break through this deadlock. First, scientists of impeccable background should help set the standards for sustaining the environment in sensitive areas, and any company entering the areas should be bonded to meet those standards. Second, the public should be informed about new methods of production that can meet the environmental standards, and any development should be only with those new methods. Third, a percentage of the revenues from resources generated in environmentally sensitive areas should be dedicated to environmental activities including biodiversity sustainment, land acquisition, and environmental cleanups in places where there are no private resources that can be used to clean up past problems.

With these kinds of investments we can have an energy strategy that meets our economic and environmental needs, and a generation from now we can be a healthier and wealthier country that is less reliant on foreign sources of energy.

For more information on environment and energy,
visit **www.newt.org/winningthefuture**

Chapter 14

Getting Government to Move at the Speed and Effectiveness of the Information Age

It is an objective fact that government today is incapable of moving at the speed of the information age. There is a practical reason for this: Modern government as we know it is an intellectual product of the civil service reform movement of the 1880s.

Think of the implications of that reality.

Imagine walking into a government office today and seeing a gas light, a quill pen, a bottle of ink, and a tall clerk's desk and stool. The very image of the office would communicate how obsolete it was. If you saw someone actually trying to run a government program in that office you would know instantly it was hopeless.

Yet the mental assumptions of modern bureaucracy are similarly out-of-date and obsolete.

Today we have information age technology in government offices running at a nineteenth century pace. The bureaucracy is made even slower by the risk-averse attitudes of the inspector general, Congress, and the news media.

Finally, the very nature of the personnel system further leads to timidity and mediocrity. No amount of extra effort can be rewarded and no amount of incompetent inaction seems punishable. Especially when it comes to national security, law enforcement, and health care, we need a government that is integrated into the information age.

Principles of Entrepreneurial Public Management

For more details, visit www.newt.org
Every agency and every project must have:

1. a definition of success;
2. strategies to achieve success;
3. specific strategies necessary to succeed;
4. specific tasks to complete the projects;
5. a requirement that customers, private sector experts, and Congress be consulted as a reality check on the bureaucracy.

Today's personnel, procurement, and spending laws are a major impediment to getting the job done. A. U.S. Army division commander in Iraq told me that when he needed additional transport, it was faster to order cars from a local Iraqi who bought cars in Turkey and drove them to him than it was to order cars through the Coalition Provisional Authority, which requires reams of paperwork in Baghdad. The Congress and the president agreed to spend $18 billion rebuilding Iraq, and ten months later $16 billion was still tied up in paperwork. Only the commander's emergency money was being spent in a timely, effective way. One commander said that "dollars are to rebuilding what ammunition is to a firefight." We need to ensure that reconstruction funds can be delivered as promptly as ammunition is on a battlefield.

We must learn to separate the vital from the nice-to-have. In the information age there is always more to do than can possibly get done. One of the keys to effective leadership and to successful projects is to distinguish the vital from the useful.

The vital becomes the priority, and if there are funds left, we can spend them on the nice-to-haves. The information age requires a constant focus on team building, team development, and team leadership. It is the wagon train and not the mountain man that best characterizes the information age. It takes a while to build teams. There should be a lot more thought given to changing personnel laws so leaders can arrive in a new assignment with a core team of people they are used to working with.

On-line is better than being in line. There is no reason why government cannot deliver services and information the way that Google or the Weather Channel can. Technology should make government more responsive to the citizens it serves, and more creative in meeting their needs. This is especially true in education. For example, the Library of Congress now has a digital library with millions of documents available 24 hours a day, 7 days a week for free to anyone in the world who wants to access them through the Internet. It is possible for every school in the country to have the largest library in the world by simply having one laptop accessing the Internet. NASA is now connecting to schools to allow students to direct telescopes and search for stars from their classroom. This is an extraordinary extension of research opportunities to young scientists and young explorers. The potential to use the computer, the Internet, and communications has only begun to be tapped. The more rapidly government leaders study and learn their potentials, the more rapidly we will invent a twenty-first century information age governing system.

Privatize more government functions. Many agencies or government services could be turned over to private companies that can deliver services more efficiently and at lower costs. This would help close the budget deficit and increase the tax rolls.

Increase public-private partnerships. The Atlanta zoo was on the verge of being disaccredited because the city of Atlanta bureaucracy simply could not run it effectively. Mayor Andrew Young courageously concluded that the answer was to create a public-private partnership with the Friends of the Zoo. The city would continue to own the zoo and would provide some limited funding but the Friends of the Zoo would find additional resources and would provide entrepreneurial leadership. The Friends of the Zoo then recruited Dr. Terry Maples, a brilliant professor from Georgia Tech and a natural entrepreneur and salesman. With Terry's leadership and the Friends of the Zoo's enthusiastic backing, he rapidly turned Zoo Atlanta into a world-class research institution and a wonderful attraction for the families of the Atlanta area and to visitors from around the world. Zoo Atlanta went from being an embarrassment to an extraordinary example of a public-private partnership.

The legislature also has a role in developing entrepreneurial public management. They should adopt new Senate rules to minimize holdups of presidential appointments. The current cumbersome process of clearing and confirming presidential personnel disrupts the functioning of the executive branch to a shocking degree. The legislature should also simplify the disclosure requirements that have become a major hindrance for successful people who want to work for the government. Furthermore, they should design a new salary structure that is flexible and reflects our information age economy. This could include independent contracting and part-time work.

With appropriate safeguards, we should make it easy to fire civil servants. And in effect, we should take every tool we can from our vibrant private sector and apply it to government so that we have a government worthy of the dynamism of its citizens.

For more information on entrepreneurial public management, visit **www.newt.org/winningthefuture**

CHAPTER 15

CREATING A 21ST CENTURY CONGRESS

THE FINAL PLEDGE of the 21st Century Contract with America is to "Insist on Congressional reform to make the legislative branch responsive to the needs of the 21st century." We have to find ways to strengthen and modernize the legislative branch so it is informed, effective, and responsible to the American people.

BLOCKED PROPOSALS (SENATE)

Today in the Senate, individual members can block consideration of virtually anything and can do so anonymously for three days. This is supposed to be an expression of an individual Senator's power to gain the attention of the executive branch. I support the power of individual senators as an important part of our system of government, but that power is being abused. Senators who block bills, amendments, and appointments should do so openly so that the American people and the senatorial leadership can hold them accountable.

Presidential Appointments (Senate)

The process of approving presidential appointments is a national scandal. It takes too long to get an individual through the investigative process. The amount of paperwork and disclosure is keeping excellent candidates from accepting government positions. We are driving away good people and slowing the rate of managing the government. In national security positions, this process is actually a threat to national safety. The application and vetting process should be dramatically simplified. For instance, if nominees have been through the process in recent years, they should only have to account for the time since they were last approved. The Senate should adopt rules that allow a nominee to get an automatic up or down vote within ninety days. Making it easier to fill executive branch positions is an important step toward a more entrepreneurial and more effective government. The Senate today is a major stumbling block in that process.

Judicial Nominees (Senate)

The ability of a Senate minority to block consideration of nominees such as Miguel Estrada, Patricia Owen, and Charles Pickering to the federal courts is another national scandal.

In President Jimmy Carter's day, judicial nominees were, on average, confirmed within 100 days. President George W. Bush's first term nominees took as long as 150 to 400 days or more to be confirmed. The Constitution calls for the Senate to advise and consent on judicial nominations; it does not call for the Senate to hide and avoid its responsibility by filibustering or otherwise procedurally stopping conservative judicial nominees from being confirmed. In some cases, Senate liberals are clearly blocking the appointment of conservatives to district and appeals courts because they fear they could become future Supreme Court nominees. In effect, a minority of the Senate is attempting to impose their extreme left-wing views on the entire federal judiciary by simply blocking well-qualified candidates who believe in a strict interpretation of the Constitution.

If the Senate continues this scorched earth filibuster approach, the result will be a shortage of federal judges and the confirmation of nominees who have no recognizable beliefs and no solid record on key issues. This is an intolerable usurpation of power by the Senate minority. The Senate rules should be changed so that the majority leader can call an up or down vote on judicial nominees. If fifty-one Senators reject a judicial nominee, the action fulfills their "advice and consent" responsibilities under the Constitution. When forty Senators block a nominee who might get fifty-five or even sixty votes on a direct confirmation motion, that is cheating the American people of their right to have a clear record of whether or not the judicial nominee was worthy of serving. The minority should be put on notice that an abuse of this process will guarantee changing the Senate rules to weaken their procedural prerogatives.

Congressional Micromanagement (House and Senate)

The Congress now writes too many detailed laws and then applies too much detailed micromanagement to the implementation of those laws. This tendency is especially strong in the appropriations committees.

A typical law enacted twenty or thirty years ago is more general, much shorter, and gives the executive branch greater freedom to use common sense and ingenuity in implementation. Today's laws are too long, have too many details, and prescribe too many micromanaged steps. The result is a cumbersome and timid executive branch that can't even execute aggressively and creatively when it has the freedom to do so.

This pattern is even more powerful (to a degree that has become absurd) in the appropriations committees. Modern appropriations bills are an embarrassment to the process of self-government. The amount of pork and logrolling (when one member gets a goody for his district in return for another member getting a goody for her district so they are "rolling the log" together) is absurd.

It is inevitable that a legislative body will carve out specific spending for the legislators' special interests. This has been true in every Congress from the very first Congress. Today, however, the process is so out of control that it is a national scandal.

The president should announce that any bill with more than 5 percent of its monies already specifically allocated will be vetoed. This would lead to a lot of grumbling and outrage among members who have grown accustomed to defining goodies for their districts and states, but after one or two fights, the veto limit would stand and the leaders of the Congress and the committees would understand that there are limits on how taxpayers' money can be spent.

The president should be given enhanced revision authority. That is how the line-item veto worked since the beginning of our country up through President Richard Nixon's first term. Historically, presidents could simply refuse to spend the money. The president would also be given the ability to trim the amount to be spent under the line-item reduction provision which was in the Reagan budget reform proposals and which at one time had over two hundred cosponsors when Congressman Chris Cox introduced it. These steps would reduce spending and rebalance the power between the president and Congressional budget appropriators.

Duplication of Oversight Committees (House and Senate)

The amount of duplication and overlap in Congressional oversight is ridiculous. Secretary of Homeland Security Tom Ridge discovered that eighty-five committees and subcommittees claimed that they had oversight over the department.

The amount of time senior executive branch leaders spend visiting a wide variety of subcommittees is debilitating to both the executive and legislative branches. When too many committees and subcommittees think they have a legitimate right to impose their questions on very busy executives, staff members teach executives to spend their time on trivia and to view the entire legislative process as too cumbersome to cope with.

One approach would be for the Congressional leadership to work with the president in defining which committees and subcommittees each executive branch leader should report to and work with. The Speaker, in consultation with the minority leader (and Senate counterparts), should make clear that Cabinet officers are required to testify in front of one or two authorizing committees and one appropriations subcommittee; for other requests from committees and subcommittees for their testimony, the requests should have to be cleared first by the Speaker.

If the Congress and its leaders find it too hard to limit jurisdiction, then the president should announce that the Cabinet will report to those committees designated by the Speaker in the House and the Senate majority leader and no others. The president should further announce a limit (perhaps three committees) which a Cabinet officer would report to and testify before (a total of six potential bodies). Without some decisive intervention, this system will never be improved and time and energy will continue to be wasted.

These highlight some of the reforms that Congress needs to make if the legislative branch is to become more responsive to the needs of the American people. Encourage your representatives to enact these and other much needed reforms.

For more information on creating a 21st century Congress, visit **www.newt.org/winningthefuture**

CHAPTER 16

THE CAMPAIGN AND ELECTION MESS: NEW PRINCIPLES FOR SELF-GOVERNMENT

WE NEED TO STOP trivializing elections, which is what we do when we put them in the hands of journalists and lawyers. All it takes to begin reform is to abolish the Presidential Debate Commission and put the parties' candidates alone on a stage with a timekeeper. This is exactly the model Abraham Lincoln and Stephen Douglas used in the famous Lincoln–Douglas debates. We need candidates to appear in Lincoln–Douglas open-ended discussions uncontrolled by consultants, pollsters, lawyers, and the media. Elections need to be focused squarely on the candidates.

That's the first step to reform. The next step is to abolish the McCain–Feingold Act which erected a legal maze for political campaigns. Enacted in 2002, McCain–Feingold banned soft money contributions to national parties; increased individual hard money contribution limits; and restricted the ability of corporations (including non-profit corporations) and labor unions to run ads that featured candidates. The result was an explosion in campaign activities outside the campaigns and the political parties (note the 527 ads, for example) and a more irresponsible system in which rich people ironically had an even greater impact than before McCain–Feingold was passed.

The Founding Fathers understood all the dangers of a corrupt political system. In fact, the First Amendment to the Constitution was designed precisely to address this problem. It asserts without modification that "Congress shall make no law... abridging freedom of speech."

The heart of free speech in the Founding Fathers' world was political speech. They wanted citizens to be able to criticize the government and the officials of government without fear of repression. The right to speak has to include the right to advertise and communicate your speech.

Every effort to legislate and regulate political speech—which is what McCain–Feingold ultimately does—should be unconstitutional.

The Supreme Court has failed in its duty to defend the First Amendment against "campaign reform" legislation that abridges free political speech. Legislating and regulating political speech has only encouraged the rich lawyers to find loopholes. McCain–Feingold promised to get money out of politics. Yet $3.2 billion was spent on the 2004 campaign. The anti-money reformers failed and they will fail again and again, except to make it more cumbersome and more dangerous for the average person to participate in the campaign process.

Moreover, while McCain–Feingold makes political activity a legal minefield, it exempts the news media, giving the media another advantage over every other citizen to express political opinions. The *New York Times* can editorialize without limit but the individual is limited by law when it comes to expressing his own views about candidates.

Such restrictions on free speech disproportionately strengthen and protect incumbents.

When I hear incumbent politicians complain about attacks on their records, I am amazed that anyone takes it seriously. Incumbents have tax-paid staff, tax-paid mailings, tax-paid travel, the prestige of office, the ability to use their office to garner news coverage, and the ability to do a wide range of favors for potential supporters. They have more than enough power and position to protect themselves. The idea of incumbents passing incumbent protection legislation limiting the right of their fellow citizens to criticize them is precisely what the Founding Fathers were trying to block in the First Amendment. If this were happening in Russia, we would call it limiting democracy and we would attack Russian President Vladimir Putin for restricting citizens and protecting the powerful. For all practical purposes, McCain–Feingold is a bill President Putin would love. It is profoundly wrong and unconstitutional.

We should repeal the McCain–Feingold Act and all the other inhibitions to criticizing incumbents and instead establish a simple law that requires anyone spending money on political issues to file the expense on the Internet the day it is made, but otherwise have no restriction. The electronic form for filing should be simple and clear, and designed so that anyone could fill it out without a lawyer. It's time to return freedom of speech to its original meaning and for incumbents to put the citizen's rights ahead of their own self-protection.

We need to restore integrity to the system with a very simple law: Americans can spend any amount on political advertising so long as they post the amount on an official Internet site the day the money is spent. Open, honest reporting is the answer to honest political decision-making. Give the American people the information and let them inform themselves.

We need, however, two other reforms: First, laws against foreign involvement in our campaigns and against foreign influence-peddling should be rigorously enforced. We saw a flurry of this kind of foreign intervention in the 1996 Clinton–Gore campaign when foreign money came into Democratic coffers. This is a serious threat to our democracy.

Finally, we need to ensure an honest system of voting.

All Americans should be able to vote and their votes should be counted accurately. Their votes should not be overwhelmed by dead people's votes, by illegal foreigners' votes, or by people voting multiple times.

This principle should be easy to enforce with a simple federal law. States should be responsible for maintaining an accurate voter roll that is purged of old names every two years.

People who have died must be removed from the voter roll. People who have moved and registered elsewhere must be removed from their old voter rolls. A simple state-to-state transfer of newly registered voters can handle this with their old registration site listed.

Convicted felons must be removed from the rolls. They should be registered as new voters *only* after they have served their time and met their state's requirements for being reinstated. No non-American should be eligible to vote. When citizens show up to vote they should be required to show photo identification. When people vote in advance or by absentee ballot, that fact should be recorded instantly so no one can vote twice.

All of this can be accomplished with the same ease and accuracy with which we get cash from automatic teller machines, make airline reservations on-line, or pick up e-tickets at the airport. Somehow when it comes to voting, we have allowed an obsolete eighteenth century model of local elections to bog us down in incompetence, inefficiency, and illegality. The obsolete system is now a lawyer's dream. We cannot afford to have America tied up every four years in a debilitating drawn-out legal fight over elections.

The time has come to adopt a system of electronic voting in which you can touch a computer screen and the result is kept in the computer and printed out on a slip you deposit so there is a paper backup if the computer crashes.

The time has come to have voter rolls maintained with a nationwide clearinghouse so that everyone can be assured of an election's honesty and accuracy.

For more information on reforming our election process, visit **www.newt.org/winningthefuture**

CONCLUSION

WHAT YOU CAN DO TO WIN THE FUTURE

IF YOU ARE LOOKING for an easy, magical solution that will win the future without work or effort, then you need to skip this chapter, because winning the future is hard work, and it begins with the 21st Century Contract with America.

The first step in getting the 21st Century Contract with America adopted and implemented is to make sure everyone knows about it.

You can download the Contract from newt.org and send it to everyone on your email list.

You can print it out and use it at civic clubs, study groups, family events, and town meetings.

You can write letters to the editor advocating its adoption.

You can call into talk radio and tell people how they can get a copy of it.

You can ask your favorite radio talk show host to talk about the Contract.

You can take copies of the Contract to town hall meetings and city councils.

You can write your representative and senators and ask them to adopt the Contract.

You can ask your governor and your state legislators to apply the Contract to your state.

You can talk publicly about the Contract. Go to "speech outlines" and "speech help" at newt.org/winningthefuture and get ideas about how to structure your talk and how to answer questions. "Speech help" also has an address where you can find answers to tough questions.

The Contract is organized into a series of topics. Each chapter in *Winning the Future* has a parallel and much more detailed section at newt.org/winningthefuture. You'll also find a wide variety of tools for study and discussion about each section of the Contract.

You can join in the chat room and post your ideas on a bulletin board. As interest develops there will be webcasts about each topic area and opportunities for people who are doing innovative activities to share their successes and the lessons they've learned.

At newt.org/winningthefuture you can find other people in your area who want to support the Contract. And don't forget that if your elected officials refuse to listen, it is your right to support candidates who support the Contract—or become a candidate yourself.

And there's much more you can do. When you go on vacation, look for ways to learn about America. Go to Valley Forge, to Boston, to Williamsburg, and to Washington. Visit the Statue of Liberty and the Capitol.

You can do a lot to strengthen America in your business life. Advertise with those stations and papers that support your values. If you have a foundation or give corporate money to charities, make sure they support your values. The business money that goes to support anti-business foundations is appalling. You could also develop apprenticeship and internship programs so young people, especially young people from troubled neighborhoods, can learn about a business.

In your community, you can join a volunteer organization. From Boy and Girl Scouts to the Boys and Girls Clubs to the Friends of the Zoo to civic clubs (Rotary, Kiwanis, Lions, Civitan, Business and Professional Women, Junior League), there is a richness to American life. The French observer de Tocqueville commented in the 1830s on how rich and diverse American community life was. He went on to suggest that this was one of the greatest differences between the European reliance on government and the American tradition of self-reliance and community-reliance.

You have a real obligation to be involved yourself, to design your company compensation and promotion system so it encourages civic involvement, and to mentor and encourage others to be involved in the community.

When you see something that isn't getting done and no organization seems to exist to solve it, your next step is to found such an organization. In this age of self-organizing Internet communications, you will be amazed by how many people will show up and become involved.

If you are a student reading this book, make a commitment to study subjects that are helpful to your country (including history, science, math, and foreign language). When you are punished for having Republican views (as has happened at Georgia Tech and elsewhere), complain publicly and loudly. As a student, you have a right to get involved in student government and make sure that student fees are spent as much on bringing conservative speakers on campus as is spent on bringing leftists. The bias of campus spending on left-wing guests has been virtually unchallenged. You should also look into the student radio station and the student newspaper as a major opportunity to start reshaping campus debate. Every time the administration or the faculty is overtly biased to the Left, you should complain publicly, appeal to the board of trustees, and seek to broaden the fight beyond the campus. Left-wing repression of young people is not sustainable once it gets enough public attention.

If you're a teacher, you have the opportunity to focus young people on their country's history, to teach lessons of effort and achievement leading to reward, to fight to move your teachers' union back to the center, to encourage young people to go into math and science, and to seek real learning rather than easy grades in phony classes.

As a parent you should pay attention to school campuses, textbooks, class activities, and special projects. You should visit your child's classes and meet the teachers. You should complain if the textbooks, the curriculum, or special activities are biased and teach values incompatible with your own. You should insist on accountability so you can know whether or not your child is learning and whether or not the school is functioning effectively. You should insist on and be very supportive of discipline as the first key to an effective school, and the principal should know he or she could count on you for support even if it is your child who needs disciplining.

As an alumnus, you should take a real interest in your alma mater. If you can afford to give money, earmark it for courses that teach patriotic history and that focus on math and science. Do not support the general funds of the institution unless you are convinced your alma mater is not totally dominated by the Left (and 90 percent of today's campuses are). David Horowitz at the Center for the Study of Popular Culture conducted a study of the departments and upper-level administrations at thirty-two "elite" colleges and universities, and found that the overall ratio of Democrats to Republicans was more than ten to one.

As a voter, your school board, state legislator, governor, and federal officials serve you. Hold them accountable.

The future is up to you. As an American, you are part of the freest, richest, most powerful country in history. We owe it to our children and grandchildren that we keep it that way. If you want to win the future, don't complain, do something about it. The 21st Century Contract with America is where you can start.

Appendix A

Republican Contract with America

As Republican Members of the House of Representatives and as citizens seeking to join that body we propose not just to change its policies, but even more important, to restore the bonds of trust between the people and their elected representatives.

That is why, in this era of official evasion and posturing, we offer instead a detailed agenda for national renewal, a written commitment with no fine print.

This year's election offers the chance, after four decades of one-party control, to bring to the House a new majority that will transform the way Congress works. That historic change would be the end of government that is too big, too intrusive, and too easy with the public's money. It can be the beginning of a Congress that respects the values and shares the faith of the American family.

Like Lincoln, our first Republican president, we intend to act "with firmness in the right, as God gives us to see the right." To restore accountability to Congress. To end its cycle of scandal and disgrace. To make us all proud again of the way free people govern themselves.

On the first day of the 104th Congress, the new Republican majority will immediately pass the following major reforms, aimed at restoring the faith and trust of the American people in their government:

- FIRST, require all laws that apply to the rest of the country also apply equally to the Congress;
- SECOND, select a major, independent auditing firm to conduct a comprehensive audit of Congress for waste, fraud or abuse;
- THIRD, cut the number of House committees, and cut committee staff by one-third;
- FOURTH, limit the terms of all committee chairs;
- FIFTH, ban the casting of proxy votes in committee;
- SIXTH, require committee meetings to be open to the public;
- SEVENTH, require a three-fifths majority vote to pass a tax increase;
- EIGHTH, guarantee an honest accounting of our Federal Budget by implementing zero base-line budgeting.

Thereafter, within the first 100 days of the 104th Congress, we shall bring to the House Floor the following bills, each to be given full and open debate, each to be given a clear and fair vote and each to be immediately available this day for public inspection and scrutiny.

1. *The Fiscal Responsibility Act:* A balanced budget/tax limitation amendment and a legislative line-item veto to restore fiscal responsibility to an out-of-control Congress, requiring them to live under the same budget constraints as families and businesses.
2. *The Taking Back Our Streets Act:* An anti-crime package including stronger truth-in-sentencing, "good faith" exclusionary rule

exemptions, effective death penalty provisions, and cuts in social spending from this summer's "crime" bill to fund prison construction and additional law enforcement to keep people secure in their neighborhoods and kids safe in their schools.

3 *The Personal Responsibility Act:* Discourage illegitimacy and teen pregnancy by prohibiting welfare to minor mothers and denying increased AFDC for additional children while on welfare, cut spending for welfare programs, and enact a tough two-years-and-out provision with work requirements to promote individual responsibility.

4 *The Family Reinforcement Act:* Child support enforcement, tax incentives for adoption, strengthening rights of parents in their children's education, stronger child pornography laws, and an elderly dependent care tax credit to reinforce the central role of families in American society.

5 *The American Dream Restoration Act:* A $500 per child tax credit, begin repeal of the marriage tax penalty, and creation of American Dream Savings Accounts to provide middle class tax relief.

6 *The National Security Restoration Act:* No U.S. troops under U.N. command and restoration of the essential parts of our national security funding to strengthen our national defense and maintain our credibility around the world.

7 *The Senior Citizens Fairness Act:* Raise the Social Security earnings limit which currently forces seniors out of the work force, repeal the 1993 tax hikes on Social Security benefits and provide tax incentives for private long-term care insurance to let Older Americans keep more of what they have earned over the years.

8 *The Job Creation and Wage Enhancement Act:* Small business incentives, capital gains cut and indexation, neutral cost recovery, risk

assessment/cost-benefit analysis, strengthening the Regulatory Flexibility Act and unfunded mandate reform to create jobs and raise worker wages.

9 *The Common Sense Legal Reform Act:* "Loser pays" laws, reasonable limits on punitive damages and reform of product liability laws to stem the endless tide of litigation.

10 *The Citizen Legislature Act:* A first-ever vote on term limits to replace career politicians with citizen legislators.

Further, we will instruct the House Budget Committee to report to the floor and we will work to enact additional budget savings, beyond the budget cuts specifically included in the legislation described above, to ensure that the Federal budget deficit will be less than it would have been without the enactment of these bills.

Respecting the judgment of our fellow citizens as we seek their mandate for reform, we hereby pledge our names to this Contract with America.

Source: United States House of Representatives, *www.house.gov.*

Appendix B

Our Creator in the Capital: A Walking Tour of God in Washington, D.C.

Every American who visits the national capital should take some time to witness the power and centrality of God in American history.

One or two days spent visiting the key historic and monumental exhibits will end any questions you might have about America's indebtedness to and reliance on the Creator from whom all our rights come.

The next time your friends contend that we are not guaranteed religious liberties in public and do not need to be taught about God in history and government classes, simply ask them to take this guided tour. Advise your friends to spend one or two days visiting the great men, the great events, the great documents, and the great institutions that are at the heart of our freedom as Americans and identity as a people.

The tour begins with the National Archives where you will find the original Declaration of Independence. It is in this document that you will find the immortal phrase declaring that we "are endowed by our Creator with certain unalienable rights among which are life, liberty, and the pursuit of happiness." That was the beginning of our independence as a people.

The National Archives

What to look for:

- □ Image of the Ten Commandments
- □ The Declaration of Independence

In the National Archives—the repository for our nation's most important documents—displayed across the floor you will find an image of the Ten Commandments. The Judeo-Christian beliefs brought by the Pilgrims and others to the New World formed the foundation for our laws,

The Declaration of Independence was heavily influenced by the Magna Carta, a contract of rights between the English king and his barons and generally regarded as the first great step toward guaranteed liberties in Britain. The Declaration of Independence, however, had a clear difference from the English concept of rights—the Founding Fathers believed our rights come from God, not the king (or the state). Here you can see the original Declaration with its assertions:

- When in the Course of human events, it becomes necessary to . . . assume among the powers of the earth, the separate and equal station to which the Laws of Nature and of Nature's God entitle them . . .
- We hold these truths to be self-evident, that all men are created equal, that they are endowed by their creator with certain unalienable rights, that among these are Life, Liberty, and the pursuit of Happiness.

This is both the beginning and the heart of American independence. Our rights come from our Creator.

The Washington Monument

What to Look for

- □ Monument cornerstone
- □ Free Press Methodist Episcopal Church Memorial plaque
- □ Prayer and psalm inscriptions
- □ Laus Deo

It is no accident that George Washington's monument has so many references to God. Washington was a profoundly religious man. When Washington took the oath of office on April 30, 1789, he asked that the Bible be opened to Deuteronomy, chapter 28. Immediately following the oath, he delivered the first inaugural address:

> No people can be bound to acknowledge and adore the Invisible Hand which conducts the affairs of men more than the people of the United States. Every step by which they have advanced to the character of an independent nation seems to have been distinguished by some token of providential agency.

Eight months later, Washington proclaimed the first national day of Thanksgiving in the United States (there were earlier thanksgivings but that was before we became a single country):

> ... that we then may all unite unto him our sincere and humble thanks for His kind care and protection of the people of this country... for the signal and manifold mercies and the favorable interpositions of His providence in the course and conclusion of the late war; for the great degree of tranquility, union, and plenty which we have since enjoyed; for the peaceable and rational manner in which we have been enabled

> to establish constitutions of government . . . for the civil and religious liberty with which we are blessed . . .

Washington's personal journal provides more evidence of his deep faith:

> It is impossible to rightly govern the world without God and the Bible. It is impossible to account for the creation of the universe, without the agency of a Supreme Being. It is impossible to govern the universe without the aid of a Supreme Being.

From bottom to top, the Washington Monument is filled with references to God: some visible, some not.

- The monument's cornerstone contains within it a Holy Bible.
- There is a memorial plaque from the Free Press Methodist Episcopal Church.
- Climb the stairs and you will see on the twelfth landing a prayer offered by the City of Baltimore; on the twentieth a memorial presented by Chinese Christians; and on the twenty-fourth, a presentation made by Sunday school children from New York and Philadelphia quoting Proverbs 10:7, Luke 18:16, and Proverbs 22:6.
- Finally, there are two words on the aluminum cap atop the east side of the Washington Monument: *Laus Deo*—Latin for "Praise be to God."

The Jefferson Memorial

What to Look for

- □ Quotes and references to God

While Jefferson often stressed the importance of questioning all things, including the existence of God, his writings and governing history make clear that he himself believed:

> My views... are the result of a life of inquiry and reflection, and very different from the anti-Christian system imputed to me by those who know nothing of my opinions.
>
> —April 21, 1802, letter to Dr. Benjamin Rush

Upon entering the Jefferson Memorial, you'll find above the chamber, around the interior dome:

> I have sworn upon the altar of God eternal hostility against every form of tyranny over the mind of man.

Of the four panels inside the dome, three contain references to God. The first to the right is an excerpt from a 1777 bill for establishing religious freedom (passed by the Virginia Assembly in 1786) and a 1789 letter to James Madison:

> Almighty God hath created the mind free.... All attempts to influence it by temporal punishments, or burthens... are a departure from the plan of the Holy Author of our religion...

The second to the right is a famous excerpt from the Declaration of Independence:

> We hold these truths to be self-evident: that all men are created equal, that they are endowed by their Creator with certain unalienable rights, that among these are Life, Liberty, and the pursuit of Happiness...

And the first on the left is taken from his 1785 Notes on the State of Virginia:

> God who gave us life gave us liberty. Can the liberties of a nation be secure when we have removed a conviction that these liberties are the gift of God? Indeed I tremble for my country when I reflect that God is just, that his justice cannot sleep forever. Commerce between master and slave is despotism. Nothing is more certainly written in the book of fate than that these people are to be free.

If you get a chance, visit the Jefferson exhibit below the rotunda. Notice the lack of quotes, notes, or references to God downstairs and contrast it with what you have just seen above. It is the same Thomas Jefferson, just a different time. The downstairs exhibit was finished four years ago and reflects the increasing secularization of public life at the expense of historic accuracy.

The Lincoln Memorial

What to Look for

- □ The Gettysburg address
- □ Lincoln's second inaugural address
- □ "I have a dream" inscription

Abraham Lincoln was a devout Christian who believed in the power of divine providence to guide the nation through the Civil War. In October 16, 1862 he said to Eliza Gurney:

> If I had my way, this war would never have been commenced. If I had been allowed my way, this war would have ended before this. But we find it still continues; and we must believe that He permits it for some wise purpose of His own, mysterious and unknown to us; and though with our limited understanding we may not be able to comprehend it, yet we cannot but believe, that He who made the world still governs it.

At a White House dinner during the war, the clergyman who gave the benediction closed with a thought: "the Lord is on the Union's side." Lincoln responded with this sharp rebuke:

> I am not at all concerned about that, for I know that the Lord is always on the side of the right. But it is my constant anxiety and prayer that I and this nation should be on the Lord's side.

Lincoln's faith is prominently on display in his memorial. The Gettysburg Address—inscribed into the wall to the left of the statue—is only 267 words long, but still concludes with Lincoln's message of the importance of God's role in America:

> We here highly resolve that these dead shall not have died in vain, that this nation, under God, shall have a new birth of freedom...

Lincoln's second inaugural address—inscribed into the wall to the right of the statue—is a mere 700 words, but it mentions God fourteen times, including in this passage:

> With malice toward none; with charity for all; with firmness in the right, as God gives us to see the right, let us strive on to finish the work we are in; to bind up the nation's wounds; to care for him who shall have borne the battle, and for his widow, and his orphan—to do all which may achieve and cherish a just and lasting peace among ourselves, and with all nations.

The Lincoln Memorial was also the site of the Reverend Martin Luther King's famous "I have a dream" speech. On August 22, 2003 the Martin Luther King, Jr. Inscription Dedication unveiled an inscription in the granite approach to the Memorial—in the center after the first set of steps—marking the location where Dr. King spoke:

> I have a dream that one day every valley shall be exalted, and every hill and mountain shall be made low, the rough places will be made plain and the crooked places will be made straight and the glory of the Lord shall be revealed and all flesh shall see it together.

The Capitol Building

What to Look for

- □ Capitol Rotunda paintings
- □ Replica of the Magna Carta in the Rotunda
- □ House and Senate Chamber inscriptions
- □ Opening Pledge of Allegiance in House and Senate sessions

As you walk up the steps of the Capitol building, recall that on September 12, 2001, two hundred members of Congress gathered on these steps to sing "God Bless America." In a similar scene in June 2002, members of the House of Representatives gathered here to recite the Pledge of Allegiance after the Ninth Circuit Court ruled that it was unconstitutional to include in it the phrase "under God."

Upon entering the Capitol Rotunda, you will be immediately struck by the religious imagery. In particular:

- The Embarkation of the Pilgrims depicts the deck of the ship *Speedwell* as it departs for the New World from Delft Haven, Holland, on July 22, 1620. William Brewster holds the Bible and pastor John Robinson leads the group in prayer. The rainbow at the left side of the painting symbolizes hope and divine protection.
- The Discovery of the Mississippi shows Spanish explorer Hernando DeSoto's (the first European to set foot in what is now Mississippi) encounter with the Native Americans. On the right a monk prays as a crucifix is planted into the ground.
- The Apotheosis of Washington shows our first president's ascent into heaven. The thirteen maidens symbolize the original states.

- The painting *Religion* honors the role of God in the nation's founding.

In addition, you will see a gold replica of the Magna Carta, a gift from the British government in 1976. Many of the first travelers to what would become the colonies came with a copy of this document in hand. It was later used to justify the colonialists' protests against the Stamp Act and other violations of their rights. In fact, the seal adopted by Massachusetts on the eve of the Revolution featured a militiaman with sword in one hand and Magna Carta in the other.

In the Cox Corridor in the House wing of the Capitol the following words are carved into the wall "America! God shed his grace on Thee, and crown thy good with brotherhood from sea to shining sea!" Also in the House chamber is the inscription "In God we trust."

At the East entrance of the Senate Chamber is "*Annuit coeptis*" (Latin for God has favored our undertakings); "In God We Trust" is written over the South entrance. Look also for the relief portrait of Moses.

Today, the House and Senate both open their daily sessions with the Pledge of Allegiance. Representative Sonny Montgomery (Democrat from Mississippi) recited the first Pledge of Allegiance on the House floor on September 13, 1988. Former Speaker of the House Jim Wright decided to make the Pledge a daily ritual, and in 1995 the House rules were amended to make it permanent. The Senate has never officially made the Pledge a permanent feature but has recited it before each session since June 24, 1999.

The Supreme Court

What to Look for

- □ Multiple images of the Ten Commandments
- □ Statue of Mohammed
- □ Opening session traditions

The most striking religious imagery at the Supreme Court building is that of Moses with the Ten Commandments, affirming the Judeo-Christian roots of our legal system:

- At the center of the sculpture over the East portico of the Supreme Court Building;
- Inside the actual courtroom there is another picture of Moses holding the Ten Commandments;
- The Ten Commandments are also engraved over the chair of the chief justice and on the bronze doors of the Supreme Court.

There is also a statue of Mohammed on the walls along with a statue of Charlemagne holding a cross. If you have the chance to sit in on a hearing, notice that all sessions begin with a marshal saying, "God save the United States and this honorable court."

Throughout most of our history, the Supreme Court has ruled that we are a religious nation. For example, in *Zorach v. Clauson* (1952), the Court upheld a statute that allowed pupils to be released from school to attend religious classes:

> "We are a religious people and our institutions presuppose a Supreme Being... When the state encourages religious instruction or cooperates

with religious authorities by adjusting the schedule of public events to sectarian needs, it follows the best of our traditions. We cannot read into the Bill of Rights a philosophy of hostility to religion."

–Justice William O. Douglas

The Library of Congress

What to Look for

- □ Statue of Moses holding the Ten Commandments
- □ Lord Tennyson phrase
- □ Gutenberg Bible

In 1998, the Library of Congress held an exhibit called "Religion and the Founding of the American Republic." While no longer on display, the Library web site has an overview: http://www.loc.gov/exhibits/religion/.

Along the top floor of the Great Hall there are a series of unattributed phrases running along the ceiling. On the right side (from the staircase) is the phrase: "Nature is the art of God." In back of the stairs: "Ignorance is the curse of God, Knowledge the wing where with we fly to heaven."

In the viewing area there is a statue of Moses holding the Ten Commandments. Across the room, northeast of the statue, is a plaque with the phrase from Alfred, Lord Tennyson: "One God, one law, one element, and one far off divine event to which the whole creation moves."

In the Great Hall of the Thomas Jefferson Building is a mint-condition copy of the Gutenberg Bible, the first ever mass-produced printed document. Gutenberg is widely credited with inventing a system of moveable type that eventually allowed books to be produced quickly and inexpensively, increasing literacy across the world.

The Ronald Reagan Building

What to Look for

□ "Liberty of Worship" statue

Ronald Reagan spoke eloquently and often about his faith in God and how He inspired him and the nation. In 1984, he wrote *In God I Trust*, a memoir of his life and faith. On March 8, 1983, he said in an address to an evangelical convention:

> I tell you there are a great many God-fearing, dedicated, noble men and women in public life, present company included. And yes, we need your help to keep us ever mindful of the ideas and the principles that brought us into the public arena in the first place. The basis of those ideals and principles is a commitment to freedom and personal liberty that, itself, is grounded in the much deeper realization that freedom prospers only where the blessings of God are avidly sought and humbly accepted.
>
> The American experiment in democracy rests on this insight.

Outside the main entrance to the building (14th Street between E Street and Constitution Avenue) is a statue called "Liberty of Worship." The figure is leaning against the Ten Commandments, another allusion to the close tie between religion and liberty. It says, "Our liberty of worship is not a concession nor a privilege but an inherent right."

The White House

What to Look for

- □ Seasonal decorations
- □ President Adam's prayer mantle

Since 1878, American presidents and their families have celebrated Easter Monday by hosting an "egg roll" party on the White House lawn, one of the oldest events in White House history.

The tradition of placing a decorated Christmas tree in the White House began in 1889. While it started as a gathering for President Benjamin Harrison's family and friends, the lighting of the White House Christmas tree has become a national tradition. In 1929, First Lady Lou Henry Hoover started the as yet unbroken custom of first ladies trimming the White House Christmas tree.

If you get the chance to go on the White House tour, be sure to visit the State Dining Room. The fireplace mantle contains a prayer by President John Adams:

> "I pray to heaven to bestow the best of blessings on this house and all that hereafter inhabit it. May none but honest and wise men ever rule under this roof."

In 1953, President Dwight David Eisenhower hosted the National Prayer Breakfast out of a desire to meet with the House and Senate prayer groups and unite the nation's leaders under the common bond of faith. Over the years, the annual tradition has grown to include guests from all the fifty states and more than one hundred countries.

Backed by congressional resolution, President Ronald Reagan declared 1983 the Year of the Bible "in recognition of both the formative influence the Bible has been for our Nation, and our national need to study and apply the teachings of the Holy Scriptures."

> The Bible and its teachings helped form the basis for the Founding Fathers' abiding belief in the inalienable rights of the individual, rights which they found implicit in the Bible's teachings of the inherent worth and dignity of each individual. This same sense of man patterned the convictions of those who framed the English system of law inherited by our own Nation, as well as the ideals set forth in the Declaration of Independence and the Constitution.

World War II Memorial

Opening officially on the sixty-year anniversary of D-Day, the World War II Memorial is the newest monument in Washington, D.C., and, not surprisingly, is the most secular. However, a passage containing religious imagery from General Dwight D. Eisenhower's D-Day address to the soldiers who were about to storm the beaches of Normandy can be found on the Atlantic side of the monument:

> . . . You are about to embark upon the Great Crusade, toward which we have striven these many months. The eyes of the world are upon you. The hopes and prayers of liberty-loving people everywhere march with you . . .

Eisenhower and other American leaders talked often of this war as a crusade against evil. The government issued seventeen million Bibles to the soldiers with a message in them from Generals Eisenhower and George Marshall. In addition, many of the government-printed World War II posters contained religious imagery. "This is the Enemy" won a graphics award in 1943 and shows an arm with a Nazi insignia plunging a dagger through the Holy Bible. Another shows a German plane and Nazi soldiers attacking a crucifix. Eisenhower's address to the troops concluded . . .

> Good Luck! And let us all beseech the blessing of Almighty God upon this great and noble undertaking.

The Franklin Delano Roosevelt Memorial

After the allies successfully took Normandy beach, President Franklin Delano Roosevelt gave a nationwide radio address and *led the American people in prayer:*

> Almighty God: Our sons, pride of our Nation, this day have set upon a mighty endeavor, a struggle to preserve our Republic, our religion, and our civilization, and to set free a suffering humanity.

Notice that Roosevelt linked our nation and civilization with our religion. He also used the occasion to commit the American people to a rededication of their faith:

> Many people have urged that I call the Nation into a single day of special prayer. But because the road is long and the desire is great, I ask that our people devote themselves in a continuance of prayer. As we rise to each new day, and again when each day is spent, let words of prayer be on our lips, invoking Thy help to our efforts.

In the radio address, we see that Roosevelt also knew how our faith bound us together as a country:

> And, O Lord, give us Faith. Give us Faith in Thee; Faith in our sons; Faith in each other; Faith in our united crusade. Let not the keenness of our spirit ever be dulled. Let not the impacts of temporary events, of temporal matters of but fleeting moment let not these deter us in our unconquerable purpose.
>
> Thy will be done, Almighty God. Amen.

This recently constructed memorial is noticeably devoid of references to our Creator, despite Roosevelt's obvious belief in the importance of the nation's belief in God during the War. *Faith* is mentioned in two areas, however:

To the right of the first waterfall, you can see this inscription:

> In these days of difficulty, we Americans everywhere must and shall choose the path of social justice . . . the path of faith, the path of hope, and the path of love toward our fellow men.

As you leave the memorial, the last quotation on the wall reads "Freedom of speech; Freedom of worship; Freedom from want; Freedom from fear." It's from his 1941 State of the Union address and shows the value he places on our nation's religious liberty.

Arlington National Cemetery

Arlington National Cemetery offers a breathtaking view of nature, architecture, and our country's strong Judeo-Christian belief system. There are hundreds upon hundreds of memorials and graves decorated with religious imagery.

One of the most famous is the eternal flame of President John F. Kennedy's memorial and tomb. Inscribed upon it is his famous 1961 inaugural address, during which he declared we should "ask not what your country can do for you; ask what you can do for your country." The address concludes:

> With a good conscience our only sure reward, with history the final judge of our deeds, let us go forth to lead the land we love, asking His Blessing and his help but knowing that here on earth, God's work must truly be our own.

As you absorb the breathtaking and awe-inspiring scenery, reflect on the bravery of those who sacrificed their lives to defend the proud traditions and deeply held beliefs of this country. In the future, what will they be fighting for?

> In the beauty of the lilies Christ was born across the sea, With a glory in His bosom that transfigures you and me: As He died to make men holy, let us die to make men free, While God is marching on.

Acknowledgments

NOTHING I DO CREATIVELY could be done without the support of three institutions: The American Enterprise Institute and its leader, Chris DeMuth, the Center for Health Transformation and its leader, Nancy Desmond, and Gingrich Communications and its leader, Kathy Lubbers (who is also my daughter). These three institutions have created the environment and the support within which over the last six years I have been able to work on the ideas that are outlined in *Winning the Future*.

I want to thank Vice President Dick Cheney, Secretary of Defense Don Rumsfeld, Secretary of State Colin Powell, former Director of the Central Intelligence Agency George Tenet, National Security Advisor Condi Rice, Deputy National Security Advisor Steve Hadley, and Assistant to the President Karl Rove for the time and openness with which they have allowed me to study what the Bush Administration is trying to accomplish. They have listened to many hours of my ideas and suggestions about how to accomplish those goals. This book is much enriched by their support over the last four years.

It is impossible to thank all the men and women in the military and in the intelligence community who have helped me better understand our national security needs. However, the contributions of Admiral Ed Giambastiani, General Tommy Franks, Lieutenant General Mike DeLong, General John Abizaid, Lieutenant General Dave Petraeus, Major John Nagl, and Lieutenant Commander Mark Kester have been especially important. In thinking about national security, the decade long friendship and mentoring of General Chuck Boyd and the support and guidance of Joan Dempsey, Steve Cambone, and Charlie Allen have been extremely helpful. Mike Scheuer has forced me to think about issues in ways I had never approached them.

In working on health issues, the support and friendship of Secretary Tommy Thompson have been invaluable. The advice of Mark McClellan, Tom Scully, David Brailer, Carolyn Clancy, and Julie Gerberding has been exceptional. The courage and determination of Andy von Eschenbach at the National Cancer Institute and the support of Elias Zerhouni at the National Institutes of Health have opened many new pathways of thought. On health matters, there is no finer leader than Senator Bill Frist. Dean Rosen and Liz Scanlon on his staff have been especially supportive. On all federal matters, Dana Haza at AEI has been an extraordinary partner. Carol Hughes Novak and her son Jonathan have, over the years, taught me a great deal about the challenges and courage required to turn disabilities into capabilities.

"The Book Team" that worked on the entire project was led by Kathy Lubbers. For thirty-two years my primary mentor has been Steve Hanser and once again he has been at the center of the project. Commander Bill Sanders has been extremely effective during his fellowship at AEI and made significant contributions to this book. I do virtually nothing without the advice and involvement of my friend and attorney, Randy Evans, and without him this book might not have been written. My daughter, Jackie Cushman, has given me the joy of two grandchildren to whom this book is dedicated and has been an extraordinary planner in developing my activities over the last few years. Her contributions to this project are greatly appreciated.

Amy Pearman and Ted Dove have been with the book project since its inception and have managed it with outstanding efficiency and perseverance.

Peter Oppenheim, Rick Tyler, and Joe DeSantis have contributed to the developing, editing and fact checking of this book.

A debt of gratitude to Peter Ferrara, Economist and Senior Policy Adviser at the Institute for Policy Innovation, who developed the intellectual framework for the reform ideas contained in the Social Security chapter.

Regnery Publishing, and especially Rowena Itchon and Marji Ross have been tremendous. Their professionalism and insights into the nature of the conservative movement have enriched my writing experience.

The Center for Health Transformation, consisting of Nancy Desmond, Anne Woodbury, Vince Haley, Amy Nyhuis, Sarah Murphy, Melissa Ferguson, and Laura Linn, has provided numerous contributions on health.

None of this would have been scheduled and implemented without the steadfast assistance of Sonya Harrison.

Valuable research was provided by my interns Chris Allen, Peter Barth, Mary Guese, Christy Hentges, Mark Morse, and John Ward.

In addition, we had extraordinary insight from Senator Jon Kyl, Senator Trent Lott, Senator Jim Talent, Director of Office of Personnel Management Kay Coles James, former Congressman J.C. Watts, Rita Colwell former Director of the National Science Foundation,

John Fonte of the Hudson Institute, Samuel P. Huntington, Albert J. Weatherhead III University Professor and Chairman of the Harvard Academy of International and Area Studies, Terry Maple of Georgia Tech and formerly the Director of Zoo Atlanta, Ken Kies, Bishop Keith Butler, Dr. Melvin Steely, Terry Balderson, and from the American Enterprise Institute, my colleagues, Karlyn Bowman, David Gerson, Steve Hayward, Michael Novak, and Norm Ornstein.

Finally, I want to thank my wife, Callista, who has supported endless hours of writing and editing and endured the mounds of paper that reflect my style. Her encouragement and enthusiasm have enabled me to focus on research and writing.

Notes

Introduction

1 Samuel Huntington, *Who Are We? The Challenges to America's National Identity*, New York: Simon & Schuster, 2004, 52.

2 Ibid., 72.

3 Gallup Poll, March 9, 2004.

Chapter One: Will We Survive?

1 *The 9/11 Commission Report: Final Report of the National Commission on Terrorist Attacks Upon the United States,* New York: W.W. Norton, 2004, 362.

2 *Report of the Commission to Assess the Threat to the United States from Electromagnetic Pulse (EMP) Attack*, Volume I, Executive Report 2004, 2.

3 *New World Coming: American Security in the 21st Century: Major Themes and Implications, The Phase I Report on the Emerging Global Security Environment for the First Quarter of the 21st Century*, The United States Commission on National Security in the 21st Century, September 15, 1999.

4 *The 9/11 Commission Report*, 380.

5 President George W. Bush, "Address to a Joint Session of Congress and the American People," September 20, 2001.

6 President George W. Bush, "Remarks from the USS *Abraham Lincoln* at Sea Off the Coast of San Diego, California," May 1, 2003.

7 Donald Macintyre, "Psst. Wanna Nuke?" *Time*, March 3, 2003.

8 Richard Miniter, *Shadow War: The Untold Story of How Bush Is Winning the War on Terror,* Washington, D.C.: Regnery, 2004.

9 Rachel Ehrenfeld, "Iran's Growing Threat," *Frontline,* July 23, 2004.

10 Thomas McInerney and Paul Vallely, *Endgame: The Blueprint for Victory in the War on Terror*, Washington, D.C.: Regnery, 2004.

11 President George W. Bush, "U.S. Air Force Commencement Address," June 2, 2004.

12 President George W. Bush, "Remarks at the Oak Ridge National Laboratory." Oak Ridge, Tennessee, July 12, 2004.

13 Shyam Bhatia and Daniel McGrory, *Brighter than the Baghdad Sun: Saddam Hussein's Nuclear Threat to the United States,* Washington, D.C.: Regnery, 2000.

14 *The 9/11 Commission Report*, 105.

15 *The 9/11 Commission Report,* 93.

16 Lieutenant General Michael DeLong (USMC, retired) with Noah Lukeman, *Inside CentCom: The Unvarnished Truth about the Wars in Afghanistan and Iraq,* Washington, D.C.: Regnery, 2004.

17 McInerney and Vallely, *Endgame.*

Chapter Two: SOCIAL SECURITY PROSPERITY

1 The calculation assumes that the husband is age forty and earning $40,000 and his wife earns $30,000. They both entered the work force at age twenty-three and the husband earned $20,200 and the wife earned $15,150 their first year of work and received average salary increases throughout their working lives). The calculation also assumes that they had been investing two-thirds of their personal investment accounts in stocks and one third in bonds that earned standard, long-term, market returns over their working years. This study was done by Peter Ferara of the Institute for Policy Innovation.

2 These polls are reviewed in Peter Ferrara, "Short-circuiting the Third Rail: Social Security Personal Accounts and the Traditional Family," *Family Policy Review*, Vol. 1, No. 1, Spring 2003.

3 John Zogby, et al., *Public Opinion and Private Accounts: Measuring Risk and Confidence in Rethinking Social Security*, SSP. No. 29, January 6, 2003, 2.

4 Remarks by former President William J. Clinton at the Democratic Leadership Council, New York University, December 3, 2002, New Democrats Online, www.ndol.org.

5 "A Chance for Discussion," *Washington Post*, December 2, 2002, A20.

6 The 2004 Annual Report of the Board of Trustees of the Federal Old-Age and Survivors Insurance and Disability Insurance Trust Funds, March 23, 2004.

7 2004 Trustees' Report, Table IV. B1.

8 Of course, during market downturns the assets saved in a fully funded system can fall below this ideal point of full funding. That would require some extra funds to get the system back to complete full funding, which most likely would come from the higher returns when the markets rebound. But in a fully funded savings and investment system, there is always a huge store of real funds in any event, far more than enough to pay the promised benefits at any point.

9 2004 Trustees' Report, Table V. A1.

10 2004 Trustees' Report, Table V. A3.

11 Ibid.

12 Ibid.

13 2004 Trustees' Report, Table IV. B2.

14 Ibid.

15 Peter Ferrara and Michael Tanner, *A New Deal for Social Security*, Washington D.C.: Cato Institute, 1998, 72-73.

16 *Stocks, Bonds, Bills and Inflation*, 2002 Yearbook, Chicago: Ibbotson Associates Inc., 2003.

17 Ibid.

18 Ferrara and Tanner, 73.

19 This assumes administrative costs of 25 basis points. The chief actuary of Social Security assumes the same for personal account plans, based on the most realistic studies.

20 Ferrara and Tanner, Chapter 4.

21 William W. Beach and Gareth G. Davis, "Social Security's Rate of Return, A Report of the Heritage Center for Data Analysis," Washington, D.C., No. CDA98-01, January 15, 1998.

22 Ferrara and Tanner, Table 4.6, 78.

23 Ferrara and Tanner, 101.

24 Beach and Davis, Table 1, 8.

25 Ibid.

26 Naomi Lopez Bauman, "Hispanic Americans' Growing Stake in Social Security Reform," Heritage Foundation Backgrounder No. 1465, August 22, 2001, 1.

27 Ibid., 4.

28 Martin Feldstein, "The Missing Piece in Policy Analysis: Social Security Reform" American Economic Review, Vol. 86, May 1996, 1.

29 For the net increase in savings and investment to occur, the government must also not completely offset it by the means it uses to finance the transition to the new system. The study for the Institute for Policy Innovation proposes transition financing that would avoid that problem. Ibid.

30 The major components of the Ryan-Sununu bill include:

- Out of the 12.4 percent Social Security payroll tax, workers would be free to choose to shift to personally owned, individual accounts, 10 percent on the first $10,000 in wages each year, and 5 percent on all wages above that, up to the maximum Social Security taxable income. This creates a progressive structure, with lower income workers able to contribute a higher percentage of their payroll taxes to the accounts and higher income workers able to contribute a slightly lower percentage. The average account contribution among all workers would be 6.4 percent, while the employee share of the payroll tax is 6.2 percent.
- Benefits payable from the tax-free accounts would substitute for a portion of Social Security benefits based on the degree to which workers exercised the account option over their careers. Workers exercising the personal accounts would receive Benefit Recognition Bonds guaranteeing them the payment of Social Security retirement benefits based on the past taxes they have already paid into the program. Workers would then also receive in addition the benefits payable through the personal accounts.
- Workers choose investments by picking a fund managed by a major private investment firm, from a list officially approved for

this purpose and regulated for safety and soundness, similar to the operation of the Federal Employee Thrift Retirement System.

- The accounts are backed up by a safety net guaranteeing that workers would receive at least as much as Social Security promises under current law.
- Apart from this personal account option, there would be no change in currently promised Social Security benefits of any sort, for today's seniors, or anyone in the future. Anyone who chooses to stay in Social Security would receive the benefits promised under current law. Survivors and disability benefits would continue unchanged under the current system.
- Social Security and the reform's transition financing are placed in their own separate Social Security Lockbox budget, separate from the rest of the Federal budget. This means the government can never raid Social Security again to finance other government spending. It also means the short term transition deficits and the longer term transition surpluses would be apart from the rest of the budget, with the surpluses thereby protected and devoted to paying off all transition debt and then to reducing payroll taxes.

31 Estimated Financial Effects of the Progressive Personal Account Plan, December 1, 2003, Office of the Actuary, Social Security Administration; Additional Estimated Financial Effects of the Progressive Personal Account Plan, April 6, 2004, Office of the Actuary, Social Security Administration.

32 Ibid., 1.

Chapter Three: The Centrality of Our Creator in Defining America

1 Gallup Poll, April 2004.

2 *New York Times*, June 27, 2002, A21.

3 Donald Lutz, *A Preface to American Political Theory*; Lawrence, Kansas: University Press, 1992, 136.

4 M. Riccards, *A Republic, If You Can Keep It,* Greenwood Press, 1987.

5 Margaret Baynard Smith, *Reminiscence: 1837*, from Library of Congress website exhibit, "Religion in America," http://lcweb.loc.gov/exhibits/religion/religion.html

6 Congress of the Confederation, 1787.

7 Reply to Baptist Address, 1807.

8 Here according to the *Annals of Congress: First Congress, First Session, Senate* is the timing of both the Chaplains and the Bill of Rights being approved by the very same people:

> *April 7, 1789,* the Senate assembled. "Messrs, Ellsworth, Lee, Strong, Maclay, and Bassett were appointed a committee to prepare rules for the government of the two Houses in cases of conference, and to take under consideration the manner of electing chaplains and to confer thereupon with a committee of the House of Representatives."
>
> *April 9, 1789,* It was reported in the House that the Senate had formed said committee and that the Senate wished the House to create a similar committee to confer with their committee.
>
> *April 15, 1789,* The Senate reported, "That two Chaplains of different denominations be appointed to Congress, for the present session, the Senate to appoint one, and give notice thereof to the House of Representatives, who shall thereupon appoint the other, which Chaplains shall commence their services in the Houses that appoint them, but shall interchange weekly. Which was also accepted."
>
> *April 17, 1789,* the House echoed the Senate report, "That two Chaplains, of different denominations, be appointed to Congress for the present session; the Senate to appoint one, and give notice thereof to the House of Representatives, who shall thereupon appoint the other—which Chaplains shall commence their services in the Houses that appoint them, but shall interchange weekly."
>
> *April 25, 1789,* the Chaplain (the Right Reverend Samuel Provost) was elected and appointed by the Senate.
>
> *May 1, 1789,* the Chaplain was elected and appointed by the House.

April 30, 1789, the Chaplain began official duties in the Senate.

May 6, 1789, the Chaplain began official duties in the House.

September 12, 1789, the bill entitled, "An Act for allowing Compensation to the Members of the Senate and House of Representatives of the United States, and to the Officers of both Houses," was passed by Congress.

September 14, 1789, the bill entitled, "An Act for allowing Compensation to the Members of the Senate and House of Representatives of the United States, and to the Officers of both Houses," was Signed by the Speaker of the House and the Vice-President.

September 22, 1789, said compensation bill was signed into law by the President.

September 24, 1789, the amendments to the Constitution were passed by Congress.

September 28, 1789, the amendments to the Constitution were presented to the several States for rejection or ratification.

9 Samuel Huntington, "Are We a Nation 'Under God'?," *The American Enterprise*, July/August 2004.

10 Ibid., 346.

11 Ibid., 12.

12 Ibid., 20.

Chapter Four: Bringing the Courts Back Under the American Constitution

1 Robert Reich, "Regulation is Out, Litigation is In," *USA Today*, February 11, 1989, 15.

2 Larry D. Kramer, *The People Themselves*, Oxford University Press: 2004, 221.

3 Michael Novak, *On Two Wings: Humble Faith and Common Sense at the American Founding;* San Francisco: Encounter Books, 70.

4 James H. Hutson, "Thomas Jefferson's Letter to the Danbury Baptists: A Controversy Rejoined," *William and Mary Quarterly*; Volume LVI, October 1999, 789.

5 Ibid, 303-4.
6 Robert Bork, *First Things*, November 1996, 21-24.
7 Kramer, 171.
8 Jefferson, the date is 1821.

Chapter Five: Patriotic Immigration

1 John Fonte, "Is the Purpose of Civic Education to Transmit or Transform the American Regime?" *Civic Education and Culture*, Intercollegiate Studies Press: Wilmington, Delaware, 2005.
2 John Fonte, "To Possess the National Consciousness of an American," Hudson Institute, 2000. Available at www.jillnicholson.com/johnfont.htm.
3 Ibid.
4 Samuel Huntington, *Who Are We? The Challenges of America's National Identity*, New York: Simon & Schuster, 2004, 210.
5 Huntington, 213.
6 Huntington, 213.
7 Public Agenda, September 21, 1998.
8 Public Agenda, 2000.
9 Public Agenda 2000.
10 Huntington, ibid.

Chapter Eight: A 21st Century Intelligent Health System

1 Testimony to the Joint Economics Committee, February 2004.
2 June 28, 2003.

Chapter Nine: From Disabilities to Capabilities: Achieving an Active Healthy Life

1 John Hill and Dorothy Korber, "Chief's Disease Rife at CHP: Strong Pursuit of Injury Claims Boosts Top Officers' Retirement Benefits," *Sacramento Bee,* October 17, 2004.
2 "He Lost His Leg But Not the Will to Serve," *Associated Press,* October 17, 2004.

Chapter Twelve: The Key to 21st Century Success: Science and Technology

1 *A Nation at Risk,* U.S. Department of Education, 1.

2 "Meeting NCLB Goals For Highly Qualified Teachers: Estimates By State From Survey Data," Council of Chief State School Officers, October 2003.

Index

For more information on the proposals in *Winning the Future: A 21st Century Contract with America*, visit

www.newt.org/winningthefuture

For education and training on the issues discussed in *Winning the Future*, visit

www.ishpf.com

www.instituteforsafetyhealthprosperityandfreedom.com